Quiet

Conversations

Concrete Help
For Weary Ministry Leaders

Alan C. Klaas
Cheryl D. Klaas

Mission Growth Publications
Kansas City, MO

Mission Growth Publishing books are available through most bookstores. They are also available by using the order form printed at the end of the book or by visiting:

www.MissionGrowth.org

Library of Congress Catalog Card #00-191124

ISBN 0-9702314-0-7

To the children and spouses
of parish pastors.
They have endured so much.

CONTENTS

PREFACE

This book is for ministry leaders who are weary of ministry. In most denominations perhaps twenty percent are in advanced stages of career burnout. That does not mean, "I need a vacation." It means, "I would quit tomorrow if it would not screw up my retirement."

These people struggle from day to day to meet an endless list of responsibilities while enduring sometimes subtle but all too often harsh criticism. They spend many sleepless nights. They experience confrontation and conflict, sometimes brought on by themselves and sometimes not. They know they are the subject of overt gossip and whispered abuse.

These ministry leaders entered parish ministry with high hopes. They love the Lord and want to serve. They have experienced past pleasure in their calling, and yet things are not going well. Depression and despair are constant companions. Many of the things they try fail or backfire, subjecting them to criticism and mockery. Reliance on just doing the same old activities year in and year out is unsatisfying.

This book is a message of hope for weary ministry leaders. There is a way out of the misery. There is a way forward, sometimes even in the current ministry situation.

As you walk through these pages, you will identify with Paul. He is a weary ministry leader. Some of his experiences will be different from yours, but the forces working on his life will be all too familiar. Watch as Paul comes to understand what is going on in his ministry. Listen as Paul discerns a way forward for himself. Apply what he learns to your situation.

As Kennon Callahan so often says, "Hope is stronger than memory. We are the Easter people."

ACKNOWLEDGEMENTS

We want to thank the thousands of pastors, spouses and children of pastors, former pastors and their spouses, teenagers and adults who have shared their thoughts with us for more than two decades. We are particularly grateful for the often heart-wrenching candor of those who talked to us in the past twelve months about "what it is like to be a parish pastor these days." Your comments have been heard. We are dedicated to pursuing ways of easing your life's pilgrimage.

We are deeply grateful to our mentor and friend, Kennon Callahan. His insights have helped tens of thousands of ministry leaders around the world. We quote his specific words often, and yet much of the rest of what we say started with insights Kennon has shared with us.

We also want to highlight the contribution made by Ken Blanchard to this work. We had the difficult task of trying to explain complex problems in a communicative manner. Ken's many books use a style of teaching ideally suited to the message of this book.

We appreciate the time contributed to this effort by content experts who reviewed earlier drafts. These include leading consultants Lyle Schaller, Loren Mead, Speed Leas, Roy Oswald, Ted Kober, and Charles Mueller, Sr.; judicatory leader Jill Hudson; and parish pastors Paul Zimmerman and Tom Stoebig.

We owe a special thanks to Brandon Brown, a gifted creative writer who helped us raise the literary level of this book. We also thank Drew Bryan for his work in final edit and Tammy Hildreth for the cover design. Finally, we want to thank Lisa Anderson and the good folks at Whitehall Printing for their work in bringing the whole effort together in the printing process.

CHAPTER 1

Chance Meeting, Or Was It?

The clear blue sky appeared even more beautiful in contrast to the powder white snow. As they filed into the gondola uploading building for the ride to the mountain's top, both men anticipated a much-needed break. They knew "quick weekends" end too soon, but they were exhausted. Little did they realize that this chance encounter would lead to new friendship and revisiting old pains.

This was to be a day of odd events. Stepping into the gondola was the first of many that day. For reasons that will never be known, the attendant directing skiers into the gondola "buckets" put only these two strangers in a car that holds six. The others in line must have been frustrated at the longer wait caused by an inefficient loader. Lost in their thoughts, the two occupants did not notice.

Locked into a small area for the twenty-minute ride, they were glad not to be crowded, but also a bit unsure about being alone together. Paul broke the silence with the common icebreaker, "It's going to be a great day."

Without even thinking, David replied with a soft, "I really need one."

Paul felt compassion for this stranger who seemed enthused by anticipation of the day, but also appeared to be carrying a heavy weight. Paul replied, "I know what you mean. It's been pretty hairy lately for me, too."

A few minutes passed. Tops of trees coasted by in silence. Two safety patrol skiers passed below, checking the wide trails. An eagle soared above, not realizing that his search for food was about to be interrupted by hundreds of people swooshing down the openings in the trees.

Paul decided to take a chance. "Sometimes things can really get to you."

Almost talking to himself as much as to his fellow rider, David offered, "It has been a really tough year. My partner and I just spent twelve months listening to pastors, spouses of pastors, former pastors and their spouses, and children of pastors talk about how miserable they are."

Paul was stunned! Who was this guy? What was this all about? How could he say such things? He wondered how to respond. Just what was going on here?

David answered all Paul's questions, seeming to be unaware of the impact the word "miserable" had on Paul.

Not waiting for comment, David continued. "You see, we were asked to investigate why the number of parish pastors is declining in one of the major denominations. We found that other denominations are having the same problem. We set out to study recruitment and retention. But, oh my goodness."

David paused. Paul held his breath. David continued almost as though he simply needed to get the words out, as though Paul was not even in the gondola.

David softly continued. "We heard stories of harsh and abusive treatment. We heard about yelling and threats. Really terrible stuff."

"What do you mean?"

David's face wrinkled in pain. For the first time he looked directly at Paul. "In one situation, the congregation and pastor were fighting so harshly that the pastor and family left town for a week. They returned to find bullet holes in their house. They sent their teenage daughter to live with relatives a thousand miles away. Disgruntled congregation members would not give up. They tracked down the daughter and placed threatening telephone calls."

Paul shot back a stunned, "What?"

David continued. "In another place, a lay leadership meeting degenerated into a shouting match between the pastor and one really strong-willed member. The name-calling continued into the parking lot. With the member sticking his finger in the pastor's face, the pastor keeled over with a heart attack and died. We actually asked the finger-wagger about the encounter. The bully had no remorse at all. He simply said the pastor was overweight, had poor health habits, and would have died soon anyway."

Paul wanted to find some way to counter these awful stories. "Surely these are just some extreme situations that don't happen very often."

David continued. "We heard about members telephoning anonymous death threats to a school board chair over firing a beloved but ineffective teacher. A pastor's wife told about receiving a phone call from another pastor's wife criticizing her for working instead of staying home with the kids. Pastors told about other pastors not taking sacraments with each other because they differ on some church practice. One pastor got fired over what color the bathrooms should be painted. It just went on and on and on."

Paul did not know what to say. He wanted to say something, but struggled to find words. Finally he settled on, "That's terrible."

David got quiet again. They were nearing the top of the mountain. Finally, David said, "That's not the worst of it."

Paul almost did not want to hear what could possibly be worse than what he had just heard.

David continued. "Harsher than the overt attacks is the subversive stuff. Rumor mills that destroy reputations. Gossip, the juicier the better, so seductive that even people who know better get involved. It's just plain meanness."

David almost whispered, "And worst of all is the misery heaped upon the spouses and children who get caught in the middle. They hear what is going on and are helpless. They hurt so badly that many can't even talk about how bad things are. They are trapped, with no options. They give up so much and yet are treated so badly."

The gondola bumped into the summit building. The door was unlocked and swung open. David did not even look at Paul as he said, "Sorry for being so negative this morning. Hope you have a good run." David stepped out of the gondola, grabbed his skis and clomped off to the slope.

Paul just sat there. He was stunned. He felt numb. He wanted to cry.

The unloading attendant noticed that Paul was still in the gondola as it slowly moved around the bull wheel for the return trip down the mountain. The unloader shouted, "Sir! Are you getting out?"

Paul was jolted out of his stupor. His voice cracked as he feebly said, "Yes."

Paul felt dizzy as he struggled through the gondola's door. He grabbed his skis, but dropped them. The unloader attendant scooped up Paul's skis, grabbed him by the arm, and pulled him to safety away from the moving gondola.

Walking in stiff ski boots is normally a bit of a challenge, but Paul was having an unusually hard time. He managed to exit the summit building and move into the bright sun of a gorgeous day.

Paul's normal routine involved pausing and enjoying the scene. It was breathtaking. The sky was crystal clear and blue as can be. The mountain range across the valley had sharp peaks of snow and evergreens. The alpine village was nestled far below. Children around Paul were yelling in excited anticipation of their glide down the mountain. Groups of adults talked and laughed as they enjoyed each other's company. Soaking up this scene of human joy and God's creation would usually be a source of great joy for Paul, but he noticed none of it. He stumbled to the left at the top of the Born Free ski trail. He always started on Born Free. It is a gentle slope and good for warming up. Paul had not skied all winter and it was late in March. Today, this easy trail would be important.

Skiing is a balance sport like bicycling, skating, and surfing. Those who do it for mild recreation need a bit of practice after a long layoff. For the past dozen or so years, Paul had regained his smooth rhythm after one easy trip down Born Free.

Today was a disaster. Paul skied like a "never-ever." It was as though this was his first time down a mountain ski trail. He maneuvered like a beginner. He felt unsure. He fell four times, fortunately on soft powder. One fall was even the dreaded "garage sale," a skier's term describing a falling skier who loses goggles, gloves, hat, and other items not strapped down or bolted on.

It was a miserable trip down the mountain. Paul was very discouraged as he trudged into the gondola loading building for the trip to the top. Paul barely noticed that the normally full uploading building did not have a line. Paul crawled into the gondola car and sat down. To his amazement, David got in behind him. Paul had been skiing for his whole life, just over forty years. He could not recall ever taking two trips in a row up the mountain with the same stranger from a previous ride up.

Paul mumbled, "Hello again."

David did a double take at the sight of Paul by himself in the gondola car. David explained, "I have been skiing for twenty years. I can't recall ever having this happen. I skied down Simba, went for some water, and then came to the uploading building. Here we are in the same bucket again. This is amazing!"

Paul said nothing.

David was quiet for a while. Then he said, "I have to apologize to you. I have been under a lot of strain the past year. I should not have told you all those depressing things on such a beautiful day."

Paul stared at his feet. He felt tears forming in his eyes.

David could see that Paul was upset. He did not know what to say, so silence seemed best.

After about five minutes Paul spoke, barely above a whisper. "I am a parish pastor. I never would admit it to myself, but I have been living what you were talking about. You used the word 'misery.' It never occurred to me that my wife and kids could be in worse misery than I have been for the last four or five years. I love them so much. I came here to escape the misery, even if for only a few days."

CHAPTER 2

Pastor Paul

Like so many of his seminary classmates, Paul felt he had a calling from God to become a parish pastor. Paul would be the first to point out that it would have been hard to see that calling in some of his early activities. And yet he was eager to be a pastor, eager to be a good pastor.

As a child, Paul regularly attended church and Sunday school. He noticed the respectful way adults treated the pastor after worship services. Paul liked the two pastors of his childhood congregation, though he never got to know them well.

When Paul was ten years old his much-loved Sunday school teacher, Mrs. Krebs, asked to see him after class. She asked if Paul was thinking about what he might like to be when he grew up. Paul really did not know, so he just said, "Be a baseball player." Mrs. Krebs said that sounded like fun, but then added, "Have you ever thought about being a pastor?"

Paul was surprised by her question. She went on, "I can see that you like to help the other children in the class. I see how friendly you are with our pastor. I just thought it might be nice for you to think about being a pastor."

Paul thought about what she said all that afternoon. She was right that Paul did feel satisfaction with helping classmates. But nothing more was said about it.

Like most kids, he did not particularly enjoy confirmation. The pastor taught the two years of classes every Wednesday evening for two hours. The pastor was a nice enough person, but he just did not seem to know much about how to teach children. There was a lot of lecturing and taking notes, much like seminary classes. There was a lot of memory work, none of which seemed to stick. But after confirmation his mom left him alone about going to church activities.

Paul's high school years were spent having fun and feeling lost. Sports and groups at school filled the days. Studying, meetings, and just hanging around consumed the evenings and weekends. Once in a while the church had something interesting for the teenagers, and Paul tried to go as often as he could. Unfortunately, his job at McDonald's during his last two years of high school usually meant working during the time of church-sponsored activities.

Church was okay with Paul. Sometimes the pastor had interesting sermons, but the rest of the service was usually the same. Paul liked the pastor, but other than a few "Hi, great to see you today" greetings, there was no real contact.

During his senior year of high school, Paul noticed that some of the adults often seemed angry around church. After several months the pastor told everyone he had a call to another church and would be leaving in July. Some of the adults seemed pleased and others seemed bothered by their pastor leaving, but it did not matter to Paul. He was headed off to college anyway.

During his time at State University, Paul became interested in finding ways to help people. During his second year at State, Paul went to a fund-raising pie-eating contest at the Christian Center. He met the new campus pastor, and they hit it off right away. Over the next three years, they spent many hours together raising money for needy causes and arranging different programs for other students.

While helping with fund raising, Paul got to know a number of other students and found that they would often come to him with their problems. He seemed able to help them sort out tough issues and get back on track with their lives. One afternoon during his junior year, a troubled student gave Paul a hug and thanked him for being so helpful. The student asked if Paul had ever thought about becoming a pastor. Paul had just declared his major as psychology and wondered about how that might fit with being a pastor.

During Thanksgiving vacation, Paul mentioned to several relatives about the possibility of becoming a pastor. His cousin and sister said it sounded like a good idea, but the rest of his family disagreed. They told jokes about pastors and described hurtful encounters with a few. They remarked how poorly pastors are paid and how much grief they have to endure. They all talked about the way Paul's confirmation pastor had been run off by a few members who hated him. It was all very discouraging.

Later that year, the campus pastor noticed how effective Paul was at helping students. One day they were talking about how best to help a student dealing with too much drinking when the pastor asked if Paul had ever thought about being a minister.

Paul recognized that was the third time in his life that someone had asked him that very question. He had thought about it some, but never really very seriously. Paul had been attending worship services and starting to remember the Bible stories he had heard as a child. He found the stories were beginning to feel more like real events with applications to everyday life, and was able to use some of the Bible stories as he counseled struggling students.

When Paul asked the campus pastor what was involved in becoming a pastor, he first heard the details of what was involved in going to seminary. Paul was troubled by talk of three or four more years of college, several moves, and the total cost. The only way he could afford college was the military scholarship program. Besides, he enjoyed the ROTC and was beginning to look forward to possibly seeing some action, so he put the ministry out of his mind again.

After college, Paul entered the Army and was trained in guerrilla warfare. He enjoyed the rough-and-tumble life. His unit was a hearty group of guys who enjoyed being loud, tough, and vulgar.

To Paul's utter amazement, a wonderful woman named Kristin fell in love with him. She seemed to see more in Paul than just a tough guy. She told him how much she liked his tender heart and that Paul was the man for her. They were married at the midpoint in Paul's three-year hitch.

Although he loved being with his Army unit, at home Paul was a different person. He and Kristin made plans to open a sporting goods store. They both enjoyed the outdoors.

After leaving the Army, they opened the store in a growing suburb. It was an instant hit. Sales skyrocketed, income was high, and the time was right to start a family.

Paul and Kristin were blessed with three children, a girl and two boys. Life was good. The business prospered. More importantly, all five became more and more involved with a local church. Soon the days were filled with childrens' activities, many connected with the church.

Paul started to notice a faint voice calling to him from his past. He had ignored that voice for almost two decades. Memories of comments by Mrs. Krebs, the student he helped, and the campus pastor began to come to mind almost daily. Paul found his lunch breaks filled with long walks as he thought about his life and his future.

Finally, he knew what he had to do. It was clear that God was calling him into the ministry. Paul had ignored that call for a long time, but he could no longer resist. He was clear about what he had to do, but needed to discuss it with Kristin.

Paul was excited as he told Kristin about his memories and thoughts. He told her about Mrs. Krebs. He related stories about the college students he had helped, and explained the many conversations with the campus pastor and all the encouragement Paul had received. He told Kristin how excited he was to no longer be ignoring God's calling to become a pastor, and asked what she thought about selling the store and moving so he could attend seminary.

Kristin did not know how to respond. She could see how enthused Paul was, but wondered where all this had come from. Paul's life since she met him certainly had shown no signs of being heading for parish ministry. She remembered childhood talks with girlfriends about who they might marry. Never had any of them even considered being a pastor's wife. In fact, two of her high school friends were pastor's kids. Without saying exactly why, they were clear they never wanted their children to go through what they had to endure.

On top of that, Kristin and Paul had just signed loan agreements for a second store and a new house. Although they were doing very well, most of their assets were now collateral. They had been living well and now apparently Paul would have to be a full-time student. With the kids all in school, Kristin had just agreed to become a partner in a medical research firm.

Kristin was shaken, but managed a brave smile. She heard herself speak words of encouragement, but she was already starting to feel scared. She didn't know what to say, but did not want to discourage Paul's enthusiasm, so she decided to keep quiet. She had no idea what the future meant or how often she would have to "just keep quiet."

Paul, Kristin, and the three kids moved to seminary that fall. The business was sold, but not for what they had hoped. The house sold quickly, but was so heavily mortgaged that there was not much left over after paying the moving expenses.

The family moved into a two-bedroom apartment near the seminary campus. Much of the furniture from their five-bedroom house had to be stored at Kristin's parents' home. The seminary staff felt a sense of accomplishment by employing Kristin in their cafeteria, though Kristin was not pleased at having to give up her medical research career for a minimum-wage job.

Finding schools for the kids was particularly tough. The public schools were less than they hoped for, but the private schools were much too expensive. Money was going to be tight. Because they lived within walking distance of campus, Paul agreed to sell his truck. That helped for about six months, and then money got really tight. A scholarship helped, but they had to take loans to cover living expenses. Fortunately, Kristin's parents were so incensed when they learned their grandchildren had no health insurance, they paid the premiums.

Paul enjoyed the challenge of the seminary curriculum and the daily demand to stretch his mind. Even his evening job as a custodian was not so bad. It gave him time to reflect on what had been taught that day.

Kristin was not doing well. She discovered that she had to keep everything bottled up. The advice from another seminarian's spouse nearing graduation was clear: cooperate to graduate. Kristin observed that seminarians who spoke out about concerns found themselves labeled as malcontents and were treated harshly by some of the professors. Kristin was learning how to hold it in no matter what it was doing to her.

First call after seminary was a relief for Paul and Kristin. At last, Paul would be able to put into practice all he had learned. Kristin looked forward to living beyond the confines of her have-nothing lifestyle in mindless work she hated.

The call to a small church in a small town was a bit less than they had hoped. The parsonage was clean enough, but it needed remodeling after two decades of obsolete décor. The salary was low, but the income tax advantages Paul and Kristin had heard about for so long were now going to kick in. The two oldest children were entering junior high and eager to be settled. The youngest was in elementary school and seemed unfazed by more life changes.

The members welcomed their new pastor and family. They all said how glad they were to have Paul, particularly after the last two duds they had as pastors. The women issued enthusiastic invitations to Kristin to join the two women's circles, altar guild, and to teach Sunday school. They wanted to know if Kristin played piano.

The fourth-grade son fit right into his class at school, but the two older children were having problems. Junior high school students have their own circles of friends and since neither of the two older children were particularly gifted at athletics, their new classmates simply were not interested in more than a frosty "hey."

On her own, Kristin decided to throw herself into a much-needed remodeling of the parsonage. She picked out new colors, fabrics, and wallpaper. She got estimates from a plumber to replace the rusting shower in the upstairs bathroom. She even found a heating contractor who would inspect the furnace.

When the board of properties members showed up for the monthly "visit," Kristin calmly explained her plans. She could have cut the atmosphere in the room with a butter knife. None of the board members had anything to say for the longest time. They did not even ask any questions. Finally, the group's leader spoke to thank Kristin for all her effort and promised to "see what could be done" in next year's budget. The board members trooped out of their parsonage without a word. Kristin just sat there stunned.

Paul's six-month "honeymoon" in the congregation went extremely well. He managed to visit all the members and learn their names. Everyone was so welcoming. They said how much they enjoyed his sermons and looked forward to his being their pastor. He learned about all the boards and committees and showed up at all their meetings.

Paul's life seemed to be going well and was filled with important activities. Paul was at meetings every evening. His weekends were usually involved with church activities, sometimes including cleaning the church bathrooms prior to Sunday services. Even his day off was usually taken with "just this once" requests to visit this member or talk to that relative. Paul was down to three meals a week with his family. The children often did not see their dad for four or five days in a row.

Kristin was in trouble. The women of the church demanded her participation in nearly everything, but they shunned all her ideas. They looked at her funny if her youngest son made any noise in church. They seemed upset whenever she suggested the need to update the parsonage. Unfortunately, Kristin did not notice that the parsonage décor matched that of the homes of long-term members.

After about a year, Kristin could not take it anymore. She took a part-time job in the office at a canning plant two towns away. She felt better, but noticed that fewer and fewer of the church's women talked to her much after that. Fortunately, Kristin had found one other working mother her age in the congregation in whom she could confide her concerns.

The summer prior to their third year, Paul received an unusual invitation. A buddy from his Army days was now in charge of a unit stationed in the remote Alaskan wilderness. They wanted a chaplain to develop ways of providing ministerial care to personnel in remote bases. Since Paul had to do his two-week summer reserve duty anyway, the congregation's elders agreed that he could help out in Alaska.

It took Paul three days to reach the remote outpost. Flying to Anchorage took a whole day, a cargo plane to the Army post took the second day, and then several hours in the weekly supply helicopter consumed the third day. It was not the end of the world, but Paul could see it from there.

On Monday of the second week, the congregation president's wife suffered a ruptured appendix and was rushed to the hospital. The family placed an emergency call to Paul asking that he return immediately to be with the ailing woman. Paul asked about her condition and was told the danger had passed. Paul explained that there were no roads and that the only way out was the supply helicopter on Friday. He would be back home on Sunday and would visit her after worship.

What Paul found upon his return was a hostile congregation. Nobody talked to him after the service. The president spoke to Paul, explaining that he did not need to come to visit his wife.

The next night was the meeting to set the budget for the next year. Paul was prepared to explain why after three years in the congregation a raise would be appropriate. The finance committee chairperson distributed the proposed budget. A line had been drawn through Paul's salary number from the prior years and reduced by thirty percent. Paul was stunned and asked what this was all about. The finance committee chair said that the elders held an emergency meeting two days earlier to evaluate the pastor's performance. Because it was less than satisfactory, they would cut the pastor's salary.

That night Paul called his judicatory leader and explained what had happened. The leader said he would meet with the elders that week.

The meeting with the elders, the judicatory leader, and Paul was held on Wednesday evening. Paul had the impression that the judicatory leader already knew most of the elders. The elders spent two hours reciting all their concerns about Paul's ministry. They described Paul as an uncaring pastor who refused to visit sick people. They described his sermons as "too preachy." They objected to his being so money hungry and to his sometimes shabby appearance. They did not like his new ideas.

They were particularly upset with Kristin. They felt she did not appreciate the home they had provided. They objected to her not spending enough time in the congregation, to her working in the factory, and being a bad example to the other young mothers about raising children. They became enraged at Kristin for being so ungrateful by being unhappy after all the congregation had done for her.

The judicatory leader listened and took notes. Paul was so stunned be could not focus. He felt dizzy and wanted to vomit. The meeting ended with Paul silently trying to fight back the tears.

After the elders meeting, the judicatory leader and Paul returned to the parsonage. Paul tried to tell Kristin what had happened, but he could hardly speak. The leader explained the things the elders had said about her husband and about her. From the words he used, it was clear to Kristin that her one trusted friend had told other members the private thoughts Kristin had shared in confidence.

The judicatory leader told them not to be discouraged. This was not the first time these things had happened in this congregation. The judicatory leader promised to get them a call to another congregation. He offered a prayer for healing and left.

Paul and Kristin sat in silence, completely defeated. They decided to keep this from their children.

What they did not realize was that their children already knew about everything. They missed their dad. They wanted to reach out to their mother, but they didn't want to add to the burden.

A few months later Paul received an invitation to be interviewed by a church in a large city. Kristin was enthused about the possibility of being in a larger place and getting a job in her trained profession. All five were particularly attracted to the mountains only a few hours away.

The children were thrilled about the prospect of "blowing this town." The two oldest were now in high school and had managed to acquire a few friends, but they loved their parents even more. They did not want to have to start all over again, but they simply could not stand to see their parents continue to suffer. Perhaps another place would be better.

Paul's visit with the call committee went very well. They talked about the need for a pastor who was outreach minded. They wanted a relatively young man, but one who'd had experience in the world before becoming a pastor.

Two weeks later they brought Paul back, this time with Kristin and the kids. Everyone hit it off well. The call committee explained that the congregation did not want to be in the real estate business, and wanted to know if Paul and Kristin would have objections to not living in a parsonage. The committee went on to explain that if necessary, the congregation would provide a no-interest loan for the down payment. When Paul and Kristin said they would not come if they had to live in a parsonage, the deal was sealed. The call was issued and the family moved just one month later.

Paul decided to approach this congregation differently. He would use the "honeymoon" time to implement the outreach activities the call committee discussed. Kristin decided to look for a job right away and only get involved with teaching Sunday school. The children were enrolled in a local parochial school that provided free tuition to children of church workers.

Within six months, things were really humming. Paul organized the new worship service. The organist did not like different music, so Paul got the elders and music committee to hire a new musician for the new service. Paul met with the evangelism committee to examine new ideas, and made sure that committee meeting nights were changed so he could attend all the meetings and ensure that everything was done properly.

Paul noticed that once in a while some of the members exchanged harsh words with each other. But these situations quickly dissipated when Paul reminded them that they were Christians and that he would figure out a solution.

Kristin found a position as a researcher at a pharmaceutical company and put her energy there. Her income enabled them to afford the payments on a modest home and get a few of the things that are so important to teenagers.

The two older children had a hard time breaking into the high school society. The oldest boy decided to ignore the lack of friends because he was a senior and leaving soon anyway.

His sister, the middle child, found a different solution. She discovered that the other girls were stand-offish when they learned she was a pastor's child. The few boys she had met stopped talking to her after they learned her father was a pastor. One boy told her that "preacher's kids are no fun."

She decided to solve her problem. Counterculture clothes, multicolored hair, piercing several visible body parts, and passing out joints solved her problem. She found that the wilder she behaved, the more attention she received. Her dad was installing all the new programs at church, her mom was throwing herself into her work, her older brother was already psychologically moved out, and her younger brother was being a typical younger brother—nobody seemed to notice what was happening to her.

After six months, Paul began to notice that he and some of the leaders were often shouting at each other. Meetings featured harsh words, snide comments, and pounding on tables. Congregation members seemed to be choosing up sides for and against his new ideas. A planning meeting got nowhere and income was starting to fall off.

One Thursday afternoon the husband/wife co-chair of the evangelism committee visited Paul's office. They were outraged at how he had railroaded his ideas through the congregation and their committee. They listed several dozen members who were opposed to the new worship service. They demanded that he stop all this new stuff or they and their money would leave the church. Paul wanted to lash out, but he realized these two gave ten percent of the congregation's budget. Paul simply said he would think about it and left for the elders meeting.

The elders meeting was another shouting match. Two of the elders had invited a dozen "concerned members" to sit in on the meeting. All fourteen people spent the entire four hours pointing out all the things Paul was doing wrong.

Paul decided not to just take it this time. He countered the group on every objection, pointing to statements of what the church wanted made to him by the call committee. The "concerned members" dismissed what the call committee said with a simple explanation that "the call committee spoke for itself, not them."

The meeting broke up at 11:00 p.m. From his office window, Paul could see that the "concerned members" and a few elders were engaged in an animated discussion in the parking lot.

Paul picked up the telephone and dialed his judicatory leader. He apologized for calling so late, but he had to talk to someone. Paul described the meeting, and the judicatory leader expressed concern for Paul and regret for not taking more time in the congregation before the call was issued. Their prior pastor had been there for thirty years. The leader had heard rumors that the prior pastor dictated everything, but without a formal complaint he had never looked into it. The leader promised to think about the situation before taking any action.

At midnight, Paul dragged himself home and into the living room. Pinned to "his" chair was an envelope. Kristin had scrawled two words on the outside: READ TONIGHT. Inside was a letter from the high school principal describing problems with their daughter and explaining the expulsion procedures.

Paul slumped dejectedly into his chair and reflected on his life. He had been so enthused to be a pastor, but his first ministry fell apart and now this one seemed doomed. Kristin had become distant. He knew his daughter was having problems but did not realize what was going on. His oldest son was never around and his youngest son was always on the computer. He did not feel safe talking to other pastors about his problems and was not sure he if he could trust his judicatory leader again. He was exhausted and discouraged.

Paul could not sleep that night. He got up at five in the morning to make a piece of toast. When he pushed down the lever on the toaster oven, the heating element sparked, and the lights in the kitchen went out. Paul unplugged the destroyed appliance and blindly groped his way to the basement light switch. As he flipped the switch and the basement lights came on, he thought that was about the only thing that seemed to work in his life.

In the basement he found the circuit box and turned the blown circuit back on. As he turned to go back upstairs he saw his downhill skis leaning against the corner. He had not used them even though the mountains were now so close to home. He recalled the excitement of seeing the mountains from the airplane on both pre-call trips and the move. He remembered how much he was looking forward to skiing more often.

Paul went back to the bedroom, got dressed, and woke Kristin to tell her he was going skiing. She mumbled something that sounded like "that's nice" and rolled over. Paul left a note promising to call Kristin's office at noon, loaded the car, and headed for the mountains.

CHAPTER 3

Listener David

David has an unusual occupation. One way to describe it is "professional listener." He gets paid to listen. Well, actually a bit more than that.

While being promoted rapidly up the ranks of a large corporation, he maintained close contact with the church. He served his congregations by leading committees, handling the finances, and even chairing the congregation. He volunteered for committees at the judicatory and national office. The denomination's convention even elected him to the Board of Regents of one of its universities.

Often, during the past twenty years, he had been asked to help figure out what was causing problems in the church. One project centered on resolving poor relationships between judicatory and national staff personnel. Another effort investigated reasons for the denomination's membership decline and what might be done about it. A recent project helped judicatories discover more effective ways of being helpful to their congregations.

Nothing prepared him for what had, at first, sounded like a simple and straightforward investigation. For several years the denomination's higher education office had been reporting large net losses in the number of parish pastors. When the denomination's research office reported that increasing numbers of pastors would soon be approaching retirement, it seemed prudent to try to determine what was going on.

The project started as a simple investigation of recruitment and retention issues. The investigation's steering group and research team decided to interview pastors, spouses and children of pastors, former pastors and their spouses, along with high school and college students now making decisions about their careers.

The interview had a starter question. It was a simple question merely intended to get the discussion going. David and his research partner simply asked, "What is it like being a pastor these days?" They spent an entire year listening to the most heartbreaking stories of tragedy, despair, and pain. Even the people who seemed truly at peace with their lives and activities described earlier trouble, or knew others who had melted down and burned out.

The task of trying to write a fair and balanced report was both physically and mentally draining. David knew that some would not like what they read. He had been through all sorts of abuse before while distributing troubling research findings. As he prepared to write the report, he remembered a well-known reality of reporting research. When people do not like the findings, they will first attack the research and then attack the researcher.

This report would be even harder because problems with recruiting and retention were caused by something much deeper. The study uncovered an avalanche of hurtful and hateful behavior of pastors toward each other, pastors toward parishioners, parishioners toward each other, and parishioners toward pastors.

After the report was published, the inevitable happened. Almost immediately the research project was criticized, and there were vicious personal attacks on David. It was fascinating to observe that the few people who were negative about the report engaged in the same behavior described as the study's primary finding. The biggest problem in recruiting and retention was the behavior of mean-spirited people who were out to destroy others.

As David pulled into his garage after overnighting a diskette of the report for loading on the denomination's web site, he caught a glimpse of his downhill skis. He remembered hearing on *Headline News* that the ski areas out west had wonderful snow and very few skiers. He decided to drop everything for the weekend. The airline web site showed one flight yet that night. His favorite hotel had rooms and rental cars were available. He quickly packed up and headed for the mountains and a much-needed rest.

CHAPTER 4

Shepherds

The two men sat in silence for the second time that morning as the gondola eased up the mountain. David felt bad for having told Paul about the problems his study uncovered. Paul sat there in shock at having, for the first time, stated out loud that his ministry was in trouble. Finally David broke the ice.

"I think maybe I sounded harsher than I should have," David started. "To be fair, there are a lot of parish pastors who feel good about their situation. They start the day with joy and are eager for each new challenge. There is another large group who talk about ups and downs, but on balance like what they are doing."

Paul said, "Yes, that was me, but for only about twelve months at my first church and six months at my second. The rest of the time has been more struggle than good."

David said nothing, so Paul continued. "I was taught to be a shepherd to my flock. Lots of folks told me I was good at helping people. I tried being a kindly shepherd in my first church and a more directive shepherd where I am now. The first was a disaster and the second is rapidly headed in that direction."

David offered, "Yes, the Bible certainly has many passages talking about a shepherd leading the flock. In John 10 Christ says, 'I am the good Shepherd who lays down his life for his sheep.' In Acts 20 the leaders at Ephesus were told to 'take heed therefore unto yourselves, and to all the flock over which the Holy Ghost has made you overseers.'"

Paul felt reinforced by the reference to Acts. His namesake, the Apostle Paul, had led that discussion at Ephesus.

Pastor Paul added to David's list with the reminder, "And don't forget the parable of the lost sheep. I like to think of it as the parable of the good shepherd."

David asked, "Have you ever had one of those 'light bulb' experiences?"

Paul was lost. "What are you talking about?"

David explained, "You know, like in the old newspaper cartoons where Dagwood or somebody gets an idea and a light bulb goes on over his head."

"Well, yes," Paul replied.

David went on, "I had a light bulb experience on this very point about pastors being shepherds. You see, I have been listening to pastors talk about ministry for nearly twenty years. Then last spring we were interviewing a group of pastors. We asked them to talk about what it is like being a pastor these days. ·

"I can still see this one guy across the table from me. Earlier he had objected to inferences that congregations should be growing. He said that if he had all the ministry resources of a neighboring congregation, he would be growing too."

David leaned forward as if to tell a little secret. "You see, we knew what was happening to membership and weekly worship attendance of all the pastors we interviewed. This fellow had been at his church for some time now and both numbers were flat, even though there were well over 50,000 effectively unchurched people living within five miles of the church."

David leaned back to continue the story. "This pastor was agitated about the ups and downs of ministry. He seemed both defensive about his congregation's being stagnant, and offended that there might be expectations of reaching unchurched people."

David's eyes lit as he reached the conclusion of the story. "The pastor raised his voice and said that he was called to be the 'shepherd to his flock.'"

"And then it hit me," David said. "We've heard that so many times before but I never really noticed. The phrase 'I was called to be the shepherd to my flock' is always the trump card stated by pastors in dying or stagnant congregations. By the way, we never hear that kind of imagery from pastors of thriving congregations. Anyway, the light bulb lit up brightly."

David turned away to stare out the window. He knew what he was about to say might cause Paul further anguish, but he also knew that Paul needed to face an important reality.

David's voice softened as he went on. "I love the image of the shepherd. But many people forget that the parable of the Good Shepherd describes the shepherd going out into the thorny world outside the safety of the flock in search of the one sheep who had wandered off. The image isn't of the Good Shepherd reprimanding the errant sheep. The image is of the kindly Good Shepherd quietly ministering to the needs of the sheep."

David looked at Paul and asked, "Have you ever thought about the analogy of shepherd and sheep?"

Paul seemed calm and simply nodded. David turned his eyes away and continued. "What is life really like for a shepherd? It features long hours of getting virtually nothing done. It is the same thing week in and week out. The routine is broken periodically by moving the sheep to another pasture, but even the change becomes routine. The shepherd's main job is to impose obedient behavior and keep away outside influences. The occupation of shepherd is hard work for minimal pay."

"And what about the sheep?" David glanced at Paul to see how he was doing. "The sheep get told what to do all the time. Mostly they trudge through the daily, weekly, and seasonal activities doing what they are told."

"And how do you think shepherds feel about their sheep? Well, I'm guessing they don't look on sheep as being particularly capable. After all, sheep always need to be told what to do, and need to be watched closely to see they don't get out of line. Sometimes the sheep are compliant, and sometimes they are rebellious. Mostly the sheep never seem to appreciate what the shepherd does for them or has given up to watch over them."

David again checked how Paul was doing. Paul was listening, so David went on. "How do you suppose the sheep feel about the shepherd? My guess is that sometimes they are content and at other times they want to go a different way. There can be lots of complaining and lots of jostling. Attempts to strike out on a new way are criticized by the shepherd and other sheep with lots of baaaah, baaaah, baaaah." David was a bit embarrassed by his feeble attempt to sound like a herd of bleating sheep.

Paul was listening and replied, "Yes, I suppose you are right. But what's the point?"

David braced himself, knowing that what he was going to say might cause a hostile reaction. "Twenty years of listening to pastors and parishioners leads me to discover some uncomfortable parallels between shepherds of sheep and shepherds of congregations. Many pastors work very long hours. They conduct many activities, and yet describe not getting much done. Many congregations conduct the same routine week after week. Even the changes in the church year have become routine. These pastors spend a lot of time keeping their members in line, and work hard for minimal financial reward.

"Sometimes the pastor's attitude is that the members are a constant source of frustration. Sometimes there is peace, but often there is complaining. Sometimes there is a struggle over just who is in charge."

David looked at Paul and thought he saw a touch of anger in Paul's eye. The gondola summit building came into view, so David decided to simply end his tale. "Unlike in past decades, congregation members these days are not sheep. Often they refuse to be pushed around. Many congregation members are told what to do their whole life, so when they get on some church committee at last they have some real power. Add a directive pastor to the mix and some congregations are headed for severe struggles."

As the gondola car bumped into the summit building, Paul had several strong feelings. He was outraged at his role as parish pastor being insulted. At the same time he knew two things: first, he had often thought of himself as the shepherd of his flock; and second, he had experienced all the negative things David described.

Paul decided not to speak. David knew that Paul needed time to think. They stepped out of the gondola, grabbed their skis, and went their separate ways.

CHAPTER 5

Abandoning Denial

David always broke for lunch at eleven o'clock. Lines in the Mid-Mountain Cafeteria get long when everyone else stops to eat at noon. A second bonus of eating early is that the waiting lines to board the chair lifts that go back up the mountain are short while skiers crowd the eateries at noon.

David was feeling better. He needed to get some of the pressures off his chest. He worried whether or not the pastor he met on the gondola was doing okay, but the gorgeous day had finally worked its healing magic. The food looked good and David sat down at an empty table by the windows on the uphill side. David looked forward to his lunch of chili sprinkled with cheese, and a Mounds bar.

Paul was not doing so well. He moved across the face of the mountain to the other side so he would not again run into that talkative fellow on the gondola.

Paul's balance had returned, but his spirit was still depressed. He decided to stop earlier than normal, eat a bit of lunch, and try to clear his head. The gondola rider's stories really shook him up. But mostly his mind drifted back to the word "misery." Paul often found himself feeling depressed about parts of his ministry, but he had always tried very hard to keep it to himself. He loved his wife and children and did not want them to feel the pain he was feeling.

Paul was not very hungry, but he knew he had to eat. Nothing looked particularly good, so he grabbed a banana and some chocolate milk. He remembered how good chocolate milk tasted when he was a little boy. Perhaps he wanted to return to those simpler days. After paying, he walked over to the windows where he could watch skiers come down the mountain toward the Mid-Mountain Cafeteria.

Paul selected a table, put his tray down, looked up, and saw David at the next table. David had a slight smile on his face and Paul could not help but laugh. For the first time that day Paul felt relaxed. He picked up his tray and moved toward David.

Paul asked, "Are you expecting anyone?"

David replied, "No."

With a friendly tone, Paul queried, "May I join you?"

David flashed a wider smile and responded, "I'd like that."

The two men talked briefly about the day and their time on the slopes. David explained that this was his first time out this year, but that he was progressing well and should be back to his normal form by tomorrow morning. Paul lied about how well his skiing was going, mostly because he wanted to relax.

They introduced themselves and talked about where they worked, each embellishing his situation a bit, as men sometimes do. Basically, they spent twenty minutes getting to know each other.

After Paul became more comfortable with his new acquaintance, he decided to ask about their two conversations that morning. "I told you this morning that I am a parish pastor and am experiencing some stress. I was a little offended by your shepherd stories, but I wonder if I could ask you a few questions."

David slid his tray to the side and said, "I don't tell many people about the sheep and shepherd comparison because sometimes pastors are highly offended."

"That's okay. I'm really interested in what you had to say about spouses and children of parish pastors."

David appreciated Paul's leading the conversation, so he began to describe what he had learned in his recent study and from two decades of listening.

"There is a lot to tell, so let me just start at the beginning. For some people, their spouse was already a pastor or headed to be a pastor when they married. They knew their path, although few fully understood what life would be like.

"A growing number of pastors are in ministry as a second or third career. Their spouses had no clue that being the spouse of a pastor was in their future. In fact, early in life many spouses had decided they would never marry a pastor."

"That was our situation."

David continued. "We interviewed seminarians in their second or third career. They all said they had discussed with their spouses the desire to at last answer God's call to become a pastor. The seminarians said their spouse agreed with the decision to enter seminary. We interviewed the spouses in separate sessions and heard very different summaries of the discussions. The spouses used words like 'announced' and 'dumped on.' They characterized the so-called discussions as a 'done deal,' not as an exchange of views. Making matters worse, some seminaries will not even accept a married student if the spouse isn't in favor of the enrollment. These spouses were trapped. They see their mate's enthusiasm, and they repress their concerns rather than veto seminary enrollment by being completely honest with admissions officials.

"An interesting thing happened when we were visiting a city where one of the seminaries is located. Earlier, we had concluded that, deep down, about half of the spouses of seminarians didn't want to be at the seminary. Some were open about that feeling, at least within the safety of a research discussion with someone who was not an official of the seminary and who promised confidentiality. Others said they were happy to be there, though they were wringing their hands, biting their lower lips, and fighting back tears. It was sad."

David's thoughts reflected on the image of those spouses, However, Paul was waiting, so David collected himself and continued. "At any rate, while in that city, we were doing something else and met a person who worked with the new seminarians and their families. With no prompting whatever, this person estimated that perhaps half of the seminarian spouses didn't want to be in their current situation. My partner and I looked at each other with astonishment. This unsolicited estimate was exactly the same as we had developed."

Paul sat silently, trying to recall his "discussion" with Kristin so many years ago.

David went on, describing that, "The next blows for many spouses are the dramatic drop in income, mounting debt, and poverty-level living conditions. Some have to give up professional careers to take whatever job they can find."

Paul began to squirm a bit. He remembered that Kristin had gone from medical researcher to cafeteria food server.

"And it is worse when there are children. Teenagers in seminarian families are hit particularly hard by the change of circumstance. The first months are often agony and there is little help. Spouses and children quickly learn the importance of not talking about their problems lest anything they say be used against the seminary student then or later."

Paul began to remember little things that had occurred during his seminary years. He had not paid any attention to them and nobody spoke to him about them. He wondered if these memories were related to what David was describing.

David continued to explain that, "Most spouses and children look forward to finishing seminary and getting into a congregation. They think things will be better, and initially they are. But we asked spouses and children of pastors two questions. The way they answered is perhaps more important than the actual answers.

"We asked them to describe the best parts of being a spouse or child of a pastor. They thought for a while. In some groups there were long silences. The women calmly took turns in discussion groups talking about friendships and being supported. The children talked about being recognized and getting gifts, although some of the children spoke about wanting to be less visible and the problems of nosy parishioners.

"The way they answered the second question was quite different, and more important than their specific comments. We asked them to describe the hardest parts about being a spouse or child of a pastor. We barely got the question out before we were barraged by everyone talking at once."

Paul could only utter, "Wow."

David went on to explain. "Now, I want to be fair here. Many spouses and children of pastors are having a good experience in their role. Unfortunately, many are not. We had a sampling problem with the spouse interviews that turned out to be a major finding. Only about half of the spouses invited to the interviews actually showed up. We checked the worship attendance history of every congregation where we invited the pastor's spouse. We discovered that spouses from congregations with declining worship attendance didn't come to the sessions. We speculated that things are so bad for these spouses in dying churches that they couldn't risk coming to explain their experience, or the dammed up emotions would come flooding out."

Quietly David added, "I can't begin to tell you the experiences described by spouses of pastors who had been fired from a congregation. It is best to simply say they were glad to be out of that hell."

David paused. Paul sat in silence. It was starting to sink in what Kristin might have been enduring. But what about his kids? Paul asked, "What did you find out about children of pastors?"

David could see that Paul's question was considerably more than professional curiosity. David decided to offer a shorter explanation and see where it led.

He started, "Children of pastors fit into one of three groups. One type does just fine. They do what is asked and seem to enjoy it. Usually they are younger."

Paul thought to himself that his youngest fit that description.

David summarized that, "The second group of pastor's children have simply 'checked out' of the whole thing. They are aloof and disconnected. They do what they are asked, but that is all."

Paul was amazed to hear how well his oldest child fit in the second group.

David took a deep breath and said, "And then there is the third group. They act out in destructive ways. The acting out is in response to how they are treated. This behavior is more likely during the high school years. Junior high and high school students are extremely conscious of how others view them. Classmates often view children of pastors as being 'goody-goodies.' This third group of pastor's children overreacts with negative behavior, sometimes extremely negative, to be sure they are never labeled that way. Girls explain that boys will not date them after learning that they are pastor's children. Even students who are not offspring of pastors described the behavior of some pastor's children as being outrageously destructive, so it is clear they are not a 'goody-goody' and definitely will be a 'fun date.'"

David stopped and waited for a reaction from Paul.

Paul was deep in thought. He remembered the "READ TONIGHT" note pinned to his chair the night before. He had just heard his three children described to a T by this stranger who had never met his kids.

Paul made a risky decision. He elected to open up a bit and see what David might say. Paul ventured, "This morning you talked about spouses and children of troubled pastors being in misery. It shook me up so badly that I fell four times this morning on a ski hill that normally is easy for me."

David fought back his desire to respond. It seemed that Paul wanted to talk.

Paul continued. "Just now you described my children. I am beginning to wonder if my wife felt what you described. I think I'll knock off early and drive back to the city and talk to them."

David asked, "Do they like to ski?"

Paul was a bit perturbed for having his thoughts interrupted by this question. With a bit of sarcasm he curtly replied, "Yes."

David reached in his pocket and brought out a key. "Paul," he said. "I'm going to make you an offer that I hope you will accept. I own a condo one block from the base of the gondola. The people who already paid to rent it can't get here until Monday night, so it is sitting empty this weekend. This trip up here for me came up at the last minute, so I am staying at the Marriott using frequent stayer points I already submitted and can't get back."

Looking at the key and then into Paul's eyes, David offered, "Do you think that your family would want to join you for the weekend in this condo—no charge."

Paul stammered and tried to decline the offer.

David repeated, "Really. The condo is available and it sounds like you and your family could use some time together. In fact, here is my cell phone. I'm going to use the restroom. I'm inviting you to call Kristin and see if you all want to use the condo."

Paul wanted to accept and was pretty sure the family would jump at the chance to ski that weekend. But he was uncomfortable about not paying at least something.

Paul tried to get the words out, but David interrupted. "You can repay me by blindly following two specific instructions."

Paul was completely lost and braced himself, without having any clue what was coming next.

David said, "First, after dinner, not during dinner, tell your family everything you can recall about what I said to you today. Then tell them that you would like to listen to them talk about what it has been like being the wife and children of a pastor. Tell them that you will write down what they say as a way of keeping from interrupting or getting defensive. Say to them, 'It will be very difficult for me to keep quiet and only listen. Please help me only listen. If I stop listening please ask me if I need to sharpen my pencil. Paul, it is very important that you only listen to them so that you truly hear what they have to say."

Paul simply nodded, so David continued. "Second, start by asking the kids what it has been like for them. Then say, 'I have no idea what he meant, but this guy who gave us the condo says to start with your kids-only meetings.'"

Paul interrupted, "What do you mean kids-only meetings?"

David replied, "Remember that the repayment for using the condo is to blindly follow two instructions. Your children will know what a kids-only meeting is, and you need to hear this from them and not from me."

"I'm a bit frightened by this idea."

David assured him, "You have every right to be frightened. Keep in mind that your family loves you and you need to hear from them. They might be angry, but they love you, and you need to hear about both."

Paul said, "I see. It is good to start with the kids so they can go to bed while I listen to Kristin."

David responded, "Oops. There are three instructions, not two. The third is that the children need to hear what Kristin has to say."

Paul retorted, "I don't know about that. There might be some serious stuff there."

David assured him, "Be at peace. Your family is in this together. The family will take care of each other. Now, I invite you to make that call."

David arose and clumped off across the wooden floor in his stiff fiberglass ski boots.

Kristin answered on the first ring. She had been waiting for Paul's call and half expected him to forget. Kristin was about to leave for lunch. Paul's simple "hello" gave her a sense that something important was up, so she closed her office door and focused on Paul's call. Paul explained the whole bizarre day. He described that even though the gondola uploading building was full, only he and this guy were put in the car. Paul told her about the bizarre reunion for the second trip up, about running into him at lunch and about the condo being available. Without saying too much, Paul explained that this man did research on congregations and pastors and simply wanted to do something nice for a pastor's family.

Kristin immediately recognized that this day might not have been the series of chance events Paul was describing. She had been praying for a miracle and wondered if this was some sort of strange answer to her prayer. She knew the children had nothing planned for the weekend, but wondered about Sunday services. When Paul reminded her that six weeks ago this Sunday had been picked for Paul's once-a-year Sunday off for self-development, Kristin knew this was no accident.

Kristin said that she and the kids would arrive at about seven that evening and that they would be hungry.

David returned to the table and Paul said, "Thank you very much."

David gave Paul a card with the telephone number of the condo management company and the number at the Marriott. He said, "Call the management company if there are any problems with the condo, and call me if I can be helpful."

David pulled his sunscreen tube from the cord around his neck and started slapping some PF 35 on as he left the cafeteria. Paul sat there and stared at the key.

CHAPTER 6

Next Steps

David's telephone rang at seven the next morning. He was about to leave for breakfast and planned to be on the slopes when they opened. Early-morning calls always provide a sense of unpleasant foreboding. It was Paul calling.

Paul was deeply apologetic and his voice had a tinge of urgency. "I'm sorry to bother you so early in the morning," he began. "I hope I didn't wake you or catch you at an awkward time."

"Not at all," David replied. "I was just on my way to breakfast."

Paul continued in his apologetic tone. "I suppose you are eager to catch that fresh powder from last night, but would you mind terribly if we joined you for breakfast?"

David was curious about the odd request. He said, "Not at all. I'll be in the Mountain Grill."

Paul hurriedly responded, "Great. Kristin and I will see you there in ten minutes" and hung up the phone.

David was a bit dazed as he walked to the restaurant. This early in the morning he was able to pick a table near the windows. The hotel was so close to the mountain that there was not much of a view. However, David could keep an eye on the gondola, which was already being tested for a day of hauling eager skiers to their exhilarating pastime. This way, if the discussion went badly, David could make a face-saving escape.

Paul and Kristin arrived exactly on time. They looked terrible. Both had puffy eyes underlined by dark circles. Kristin had valiantly tried in vain to cover hers with makeup. And yet their brisk pace implied they had some business to take care of. David was seriously concerned about the next two minutes.

As David rose, Paul started by saying, "Good morning. Thank you so much for seeing us. I'd like to introduce Kristin."

David shook Paul's hand and then offered his hand to Kristin. She started to reach for his hand but then lunged forward to give him a bear hug. With her cheek pressed against David's, Kristin whispered. "Thank you, thank you, thank you."

Somewhat chagrined by her abnormally forward lunge, Kristin stepped back and said, "I'm sorry. I'm just so pleased to meet you."

David looked over to see Paul smiling. All three sat down and Paul began. "We are deeply grateful for all you have done for us."

David inserted himself by blurting, "Oh, it's really all right. The condo was available. I'm happy you could use it."

Paul continued. "It was wonderful for you to give us the weekend there, but that isn't what we are talking about. You see, we have been up all night, all five of us. We decided to let our children sleep this morning, but we wanted to thank you in person as quickly as possible."

Kristin softly added, "Thank you so much. What a blessing."

It was clear to David that something powerful had happened in this wonderful family of God. He knew it was best to just listen.

Paul went on, "I have a wonderful wife and three wonderful children. They have supported me in ways I never knew about. It was hard for me to listen last night. Many times I wanted to defend myself. The note taking helped."

Kristin gently cupped both of her hands around Paul's arm as she inserted, "At first we frequently had to ask if Paul needed to sharpen his pencil."

They smiled at each other as Paul continued. "The kids were surprised when I asked them about their meetings. In fact, they seemed a bit miffed. I told them that I had no idea what I was asking about, but that was part of my agreement with you to use the condo."

Paul slipped back in his chair. His voice changed to a soft and somber tone. "I simply had no idea what they went through. The two oldest talked about how lonely they were being isolated at school by all the moves."

"They even told me how angry they were about the call I received and declined halfway through our time at the first church. Kristin and I had assured them not to worry, but they told me the threat of a move was almost as bad as actually moving. It filled them with fear and uncertainty. Then later, when things started deteriorating at the first church, they knew we had to move before I even knew it."

Kristin injected, "We were careful never to talk about our problems with the parsonage, church leaders, or the fallout from the trip to Alaska. And yet somehow they knew about it all."

Paul lost his smile, but at the same time did not have the furrowed brow of an angry person. "They told us how harshly the other children in the church treated them. They told us about three times when one of the women of the congregation scolded them for not behaving in church. They described how members would make insulting comments about me when they knew our children could hear."

"It was all depressing," Kristin said. "I knew about some of that stuff, but my goodness, some people can be just outrageous."

Paul continued her thought by adding, "Right. And even those people who in their mind are being helpful often are not. It's too bad members of a congregation can't give their pastor and family the same level of privacy the members insist on for themselves."

"Anyway," Paul said, as if to return to his original point, "what really hurt is when all three children said how much they missed me. They described feeling resentful that I always had time for others rather than for them. They mentioned how often people called during dinner, apologized for interrupting, but then just kept talking about something that could easily wait for a few hours. They explained how bad they felt when I missed activities important to them to attend church meetings that later I would describe as having been a waste of time."

Paul paused. Then with a tear welling up in his eye said, "But they kept saying how much they missed me."

He paused again to regain his composure. Paul barely got out the words, "Even our daughter…" before he had to stop.

The server was approaching, so Paul suggested they order. After telling the server what they wanted for breakfast, there were several minutes of silence. David thought Kristin would help to fill in Paul's words. David was impressed with her wisdom in recognizing that Paul needed to find and speak his own words. Perhaps she realized that this conversation was a critical part of Paul's healing process, and he needed to speak the words out loud.

After a few minutes, Paul continued as if he had only paused to take a normal breath. "We have been on the verge of losing our daughter to all sorts of evil. Everything we tried was rebuffed, and with great anger. But last night she was as soft and tender as when she was three and we read nursery rhymes at bedtime."

Kristin now was able to mention, "Our oldest son told us how hard he was trying to just hang on until he could be rid of, as he put it, the 'whole sorry mess.' He wanted to be closer to his dad, but could no longer bear to see Paul suffer. He apologized for withdrawing, but simply couldn't figure out another way."

Paul regained his composure and observed, "It is so interesting how differently the children react. Our youngest son knew about how much his brother and sister were hurting, but just didn't seem to have been so dramatically affected. We are aware that denial is a problem." Paul and Kristin exchanged glances and smiles. "But he seems to be doing okay."

Paul concluded his review of the children's portion of last night's discussions by saying, "It was amazing. They actually held meetings, sometimes more often than once a week, to help each other out. They didn't tell either of us about them." Then Paul did a kind of double take and said, "But I guess you knew from your research all about kids-only meetings in clergy families."

David simply replied, "Yes, we often heard about them."

Then Paul turned to Kristin. Speaking to David while looking at Kristin, Paul said, "I can't begin to tell you how grateful I am to

God for bringing us together and to Kristin for letting me be part of her life." Now it was Kristin's turn for tears.

Paul gently kissed Kristin's cheek and continued. "She has been such a blessing to me in ways I can't express."

Paul turned back to David, saying, "She saw something in me when I was a pretty wild guy. She gave up many of her dreams so I could answer God's calling me to be a pastor. She supported me in tough times and shielded me from some awful stuff heaped on her by some well-meaning people and by others who were just plain mean. I've just been so blessed."

Paul looked at Kristin with a gaze of undying gratitude. "We've been up all night reconnecting."

Then Paul bowed his head as if embarrassed about his next comment. "Actually, it was more than reconnecting. As my family talked, I began to feel how deeply I had wronged them. At first, I wanted to defend my actions. Your reminder to listen and the trick about taking notes helped me focus on what they had to say rather than my rebuttal."

Paul drew a deep breath. Something significant was coming. He continued, "It became clear to me that I needed to confess the error of my ways of allowing the ministry to be my life's focus."

Paul lifted his eyes to look at David. His tear-filled expression showed a glint of a smile. He took a deep breath and said, "Guess what happened next."

David already knew, but he realized that Paul had to say the words himself, out loud. David smiled but remained quiet.

Paul looked at Kristin and said, "Kristin and the children told me they loved and forgave me." He was overcome with emotion and paused to regain composure. "It reminded me of the saving grace we experience in Jesus."

Paul and Kristin looked back across the table at David and together said, "Thank you."

Both Paul and Kristin seemed to have experienced a life-changing event. The food arrived and not much was said as they ate. David thought he could see an aura of peace descend on this exhausted couple.

As David was finishing breakfast, Kristin asked, "Is what we have been through last night also in your research?"

David put down his fork and drank the final swallows of his juice. With a touch of sadness he replied, "Unfortunately not. Most pastors just keep on going. They are so focused on ministry activity that it becomes almost like their idol in that they work so hard on their church activities that they lose sight of the reason for ministry and other critical parts of life. Some say that they think things will get better if they just work a little harder. Others just keep going until they drop, either drop dead or drop out. It is sad."

"We found that twenty percent of parish pastors are in advanced stages of burnout and another twenty percent are well along the way. Those are some huge numbers."

"We also discovered that less than a quarter of these pastors are getting help, and much smaller numbers of troubled spouses and children are being helped. Virtually all pastors told us they either were not aware of where to go for help, or didn't trust the help provided by the denomination or judicatory. The final bit of discouraging information we uncovered is that the vast majority of the relatively few pastors receiving some kind of help are not going to full-time professionals. As you know, these are tough issues requiring special skills to resolve. As I said, this whole situation is pretty sad."

David reflected for a few moments, then perked up and went on, "But on a brighter note, I have to say congratulations to you, Paul. You see, most pastors are in some form of denial. They simply ignore the possibility that they have problems and become more angry or entrenched. They work hard to make the congregation submit to their will on a wide range of functional details. That results in either of two problems. Either the congregation lashes out and then the pastor is forced to leave, or the congregation conforms, only to unload on the next pastor. The successor gets hit with years of pent-up hostility or aggressively confrontational behavior. Either way, pastors, families, and congregations are severely damaged."

David went on. "You and Kristin have achieved a major milestone. Pastors can't be helped until they first recognize what is going on and admit they need help. When pastors confess, repent, and receive forgiveness from the family, a huge weight is lifted."

Paul and Kristin looked at each other and felt a sense of having just experienced a life-changing event. Kristin said, "That makes a lot of sense. What do we do next?"

From the corner of his eye, Paul noticed skiers inside the gondola cars going up the hill. He asked, "Yes, we are eager to hear your thoughts on what else we can learn, but I notice that the mountain is open and you are probably eager to get going."

David smiled and said, "I can help you, but not until after you've rested. Do you want to have dinner tonight?"

Paul and Kristin suddenly became aware that they were exceedingly tired. Paul invited David to dinner, saying, "We greatly appreciate what you have done for us. Please allow us to buy you dinner at the Charthouse Restaurant."

David quickly commented, "That is my favorite restaurant here, but it's a little pricey."

Before he could continue, Paul interrupted. "Please. We want to do this. Besides, it is a good place to talk."

As they rose to leave, two boys and a girl came walking through the restaurant toward them. Paul had a shocked expression on his face as he looked at the young lady. "Honey," he blurted. "What happened to your hair?"

Kristin gave Paul a sharp elbow in his ribs and whispered a ventriloquistic order, "Quiet!" Then she whispered to David, "Her hair used to be orange and purple."

Their daughter had a big smile on her face as she hugged her dad. "Good morning. We saw your note and thought we would join you for breakfast."

Paul and Kristin introduced their three children to David. David knew they needed to be alone so he excused himself to head for the hills. David paused at the restaurant door and looked back at the family. They were smiling and laughing, as if for the first time in a very long while. David marveled to himself about the power of confession, repentance, and forgiveness.

CHAPTER 7

Trust, Perfectionism, and Hoarding Ministry

Saturday evening was a star-studded extravaganza. The full·moon gave the snowcapped mountain peaks across the valley a shimmering glow. It reminded David of the effect a black light has to heighten the visual image of light-colored objects in an otherwise dark room. The air was crisp, though not the wicked cold of winter.

David looked forward to the dinner that evening. The Charthouse Restaurant is a "sweet and sour" mixture of décor and setting. Here in the mountainous cold of the end of winter is a glassed capsule of Hawaiian warmth. The flowered, short-sleeved shirts of the service staff and well-rounded seafood menu provide a comfortable setting in which to savor a meal with friends.

Paul and Kristin were already seated when David arrived. They greeted him, and Paul explained that, "The children wanted to watch the figure skating show at the arena and take in a movie. So it's just the three of us."

They reviewed the menu, explained their selections to the server, and settled in for an enjoyable evening. David talked about how much he enjoyed the back bowl areas but wished he had better rhythm for the bumped-up mogul fields. Paul and Kristin described taking a morning nap and then joining the "crack of noon club," actually not getting out until about one in the afternoon. All three had an exhilarating day.

Paul again said, "We really want to thank you again for helping us reconnect with each other."

Kristin joined in, "Absolutely. I was beginning to worry about us, the kids, and what was going on at church. At least our family is doing much better."

Paul leaned forward to apologize, sort of. He said, "It has been a wonderful two days and I have learned a lot. But we go back home tomorrow afternoon, and Monday I go back to the office. I have a feeling that you might have some suggestions for my situation at church."

David was glad to hear their comment. It was obvious they had agreed to broach this topic and seemed ready to listen as a team.

David also leaned forward a bit and began, "There are a few things that might be helpful. Please understand that I am talking from many years observing firsthand a large number of congregations. However, I have never visited your congregation, so just keep that in mind."

Kristin simply said, "Please continue."

David replied, "Okay. Paul, you have overcome a large hurdle by admitting that things are not going well, seeing that you need help, and asking for help. It is important for you to understand that most pastors experiencing ministry distress are still in denial about it. They feel the symptoms of fatigue and stress, but deny that their ministry is in trouble. In the quiet of their study or during insomnia at two in the morning they sometimes sense that all isn't right. But being an all-sufficient 'lone ranger' pastor, completely in charge, has been thoroughly drummed into them.

"Often those who are able to admit that they are in trouble have a hard time asking for help even when the help is completely confidential."

"Paul, you and Kristin have taken an important first step," David continued. "But it is only the first step."

David paused to give his dinner partners time to comment. They were silent and seemed eager to hear more, so David continued.

"My guess is that you are not yet ready to deal with the issues at the congregation. Before that can happen, you need to address a common problem for parish pastors. I sense that Kristin can help, if you let her."

Paul and Kristin looked at each other, smiled, and looked back at David with anticipation in their eyes.

David asked, "Paul, how many board and committee meetings do you attend in a typical month?"

Paul rolled his eyes and thought to himself that it was a lot. Thinking out loud, he said, "Well, there are twelve regular committee meetings a month, plus three special meetings for task groups. I attend all the women's group functions and two of the four men's group functions. Then there are the two senior lay leadership groups, three or four for worship planning plus weekly confirmation instruction. There are one or two meetings every evening and something on most Saturdays. I don't know how many that is, but it is a lot."

David asked, "How many hours do you spend on calls to members in the hospital or shut-ins?"

Again, Paul seemed to be guessing when he said, "Of course that varies from month to month. Each visit is as short as half an hour or as long as several hours. I visit all members at least by their third day in the hospital, if the family lets me know. Unfortunately, they don't always let the office know so I don't hear about it until later or even after they have returned home. Mostly it makes people mad if I am not there right away, even if nobody told me about the problem. Shut-ins get a visit from me two or three times a year. It's not enough, but it's all I have time for."

David asked a third question. "How many hours do you spend visiting nonmembers. You know, people new to the community or visitors to worship?"

Paul sat back and replied, "Not much at all. There just isn't enough time. In fact, the members at my first congregation complained when they didn't see my car parked at church. They said I wasn't working and off someplace loafing."

David put down his fork, knowing that what he had to explain might not be easy for Paul to hear. "Let me start by saying that the three answers you gave are typical. In fact, the problem of members not telling you about hospitalization and then being angry for not getting a visit is common in a certain type of congregation. So, is that issue about being in the office? Probably not, but we'll save dealing with those two common problems for another time. At this point, I just want you to be at peace that these problems will continue and there is little you can do about them at the moment."

David continued, "Several years ago I had the privilege of attending a small meeting of people like myself who have spent many years studying congregations. We talked about the remarkable differences between struggling and thriving congregations. One of the meeting participants pointed out that none of us had ever studied or written about the simple concept of trust. We all agreed that just below the surface in struggling ministries is a lack of trust. And just below the surface in thriving congregations is a high level of trust."

"Lately we have come to see this important difference as being closely tied to a compulsion for perfectionism. This disease is in pastors and in parishes. Perfectionism is very damaging to the perfectionist and to those around the perfectionist. I'm not talking about striving for quality. Quality is always important. This is different. This has to do with a compulsive obsession for perfection."

Paul was squirming a bit but did not seem to notice. He asked, "Could you give me some examples?"

"Sure," replied David. "But first I'm going to give you a two-part perfectionism test. Are you ready?"

Paul seemed uneasy, but said he was ready.

David said, "The first part is to identify the thirty percent of your in-basket content that you can give up."

Paul laughed as he glanced at Kristin. Seeing her stoic stare, he turned his laugh back to David to confirm the joke. Seeing that David also was not laughing, Paul attempted to rescue his gaffe with a surprised observation, "Oh! You're serious."

David simply said, "Absolutely."

Paul squirmed as he thought. Twice he started to speak, but stopped short. Finally he said, "I could cut a few things, but not thirty percent."

David pressed on. "Fair enough. Now for the second part. Name the three to five key meetings you have to attend, skipping all the rest."

Paul sought to correct David by asserting, "You mean the three to five I could skip."

David was firm. "No, you heard correctly the first time. Which are the three to five meetings you are required to attend, skipping all the rest?"

Paul simply replied, "That's impossible."

David smiled, "Congratulations. You have qualified as a perfectionist. You see, some pastors need to attend every meeting because something might happen with which they don't agree. They feel they need to know most of the details to be sure that things are done correctly. At the same time, they have a hard time admitting that the notion of 'done correctly' really means 'done as I think they should be done.' These pastors will rationalize their compulsion by pointing out that meetings struggle when the pastor isn't there. In fact, meetings struggle in the pastor's absence because of habit, not capability."

> Perfectionism test:
> 1. Identify 30% of in-basket you can give up.
> 2. Name 3-5 meetings you *must* attend, skipping the rest.

Paul's discomfort was clear in his body language. With a tone of protest he injected, "Yes, but mistakes will be made if the pastor doesn't keep track of everything."

Kristin gently touched Paul's arm and asked, "Would you like me to sharpen your pencil?"

Since he was not taking written notes, Paul seemed a bit agitated by the question. Fortunately his face quickly flashed a smile at Kristin's gentle reminder of the importance of listening rather than thinking about being defensive.

Paul settled back into his chair and David knew he could continue. "Let me give you two examples. First Church asked us to help them find a way to make decisions more rapidly. Many details were getting bogged down and the whole ministry was stagnating. It is unusual for a large and outwardly stable church to ask for help, but both the senior pastor and the lay leaders recognized there was a problem that seemed to be holding back the ministry. The senior pastor told us his in-basket contained four-month-old requests by outside groups to use the building. He agreed that a simple building usage policy could be developed, and his competent administrative assistant could handle the requests. When we returned four months later, the senior pastor was now five months behind in responding to building usage requests."

Paul suggested, "It sounds like he was so busy he didn't even have time to develop the policy."

David countered, "That is what a perfectionist would observe about the situation."

Paul looked like he wanted to object, but stopped when Kristin again touched his arm. Paul smiled at her and said, "Looks like you got me again."

They both smiled and turned back to David, "Two things were actually happening. First, the senior pastor had lots of people in his congregation who could develop an effective policy in only one two-hour meeting. Second, he simply didn't understand that his perfectionism was so severe that he couldn't even recognize that he didn't need to develop the policy. Deep down he couldn't bring himself to give up control."

Paul was listening, but David could see that the light bulb had not yet come on.

David decided he needed to elaborate on this critical point that is so hard for perfectionists to see in themselves. "Let me tell you about two parts of a discussion with First Church's paid staff that occurred earlier in the day. We asked how the new computer system was working out at First Church. All dozen staff members said it was hard and they didn't know what they were doing. We asked how they planned to solve that problem. They said nobody had time to deal with the agony of selecting a training vendor or the torture of learning new software."

Kristin inserted, "I've been through that."

Paul agreed as David continued. "We simply asked if First Church had any teenagers in the congregation. They replied that there were hundreds. We asked if any of these teens knew anything about computers. Practically in unison the group responded that almost all of the teens knew computers. We paused for effect as one, then another, then a third person recognized where these questions were leading. We then asked if each staff person would like to have one or two computer system tutors, available day or night, at no cost to the congregation. Everyone laughed as they realized that they had resources to solve this problem right under their noses."

Paul was fascinated as he observed, "What a great story. I bet it happens all the time."

Kristin added, "That was a helpful lesson for them to learn."

David had a sly smile as he went on, "You would think so, wouldn't you? The meeting continued and about ten minutes later we asked why First Church didn't have a web site. The senior pastor explained he had not had time to find a web site provider, hire a designer, or allocate money in next year's budget. We asked again asked if there were any teenagers in First Church who had personal web sites. The youth counselor guessed that two or three dozen did. We said nothing as the room burst into laughter."

David had a big smile as he recalled the scene at First Church. Kristin beamed as she savored the incident, but Paul was not enjoying the story.

Paul recognized where David's story was leading and had some serious concerns. With troubled eyes, Paul asserted, "That's fine for something like that, but most congregations have a real hard time getting people to volunteer."

David decided to be direct and looked straight into Paul's eyes, saying, "That is what a perfectionist who has low levels of trust in members would feel. Even the smallest congregations have large amounts of untapped resources, but not for things that no longer have meaning to people. Most congregations have way too many boards and committees with far too many members on each. Most congregations take much too long to make relatively few decisions. In most cases, one or two people can make good decisions quickly. When large numbers of people are involved in making minor decisions, it slows the whole ministry down. In fact, tens of thousands of congregations have become so paralyzed about doing anything different, they are forced to limit their activities to those which have been in place for twenty or thirty years. Their ministries are shrinking and they blame outside forces rather than face their habits as a primary cause of their problems."

David leaned back but did not offer Paul an opening to speak. "Outwardly, these issues seem lodged in the congregation. We can get to that at a later time. The important point tonight is that 'people lead the way they experience being led.'"

David repeated this key observation by reflecting, "Our mentor, Kennon Callahan, was particularly helpful in pointing out that 'people lead the way they experience being led.'"

David stopped to see how Paul and Kristin were doing. Both were thinking, so David provided a contrasting story. "Let me tell you about high trust in a thriving Great Commission congregation. The church's senior pastor told us about a trip to the church office with his daughter to retrieve a book he wanted to read that evening. She pointed to one item on the poster listing that day's activities at the church and asked what that activity was all about. The senior pastor explained how that simple question led to two insights. First, the senior pastor realized he didn't know what the activity was, and second, he realized he didn't feel any need to know what the activity was."

Paul instantly protested, "How can a pastor not know what is going on in the congregation?"

David shot back, but being careful to speak softly, "This pastor knows the critical elements of the thriving ministry, but does not need to know the content of all programs or be involved in determining the color of the bathrooms. This ministry thrives because the pastor trusts members to make decisions. More members making more decisions means the ministry can be more effective as a mission outpost."

Paul sat back and continued to object to the logic of David's assertion. "But how are they sure that mistakes don't happen?"

David honed in on the key issue. "Mistakes are celebrated, not avoided."

Paul was confused and objected with a stern, "What!"

David smiled and replied with what at first seemed to Paul as an absurd observation. David said, "You two have raised three wonderful children." Paul seemed completely lost, but Kristin was catching on.

David pointed out that, "As you raised your children you gave them the freedom to make decisions, knowing that some would not work out."

Kristin helped by commenting, "That is how children grow."

David explained, "The same is true for members of congregations. Growth occurs when people have an opportunity to grow. Growth does not occur by being told what to think and what to do. Instruction is helpful to provide a base of knowledge, but it does not provide practice."

> ## If the pastor does not trust the members, how can members trust the pastor?

David added emphasis to his next thoughts. "Remember, people lead the way they experience being led. If people are not trusted, they will not exhibit trust. That is why members are suspicious when the pastor's car isn't at the office. Conflict is inevitable when everybody is watching and second guessing-everybody else. That is at the heart of why members attack pastors, pastors have negative feelings about members, and everyone is in a constant state of struggle."

Paul closed his eyes and reflected. Everything he had just heard was the opposite of what he had been taught and thought about pastoring a congregation.

David softly said, "Many pastors can't understand this because it is the opposite of how they visualize being a pastor."

Paul was not surprised that David spoke what Paul was thinking. It was hard to give up control and just listen and reflect.

David decided to take a chance. He drew himself closer to Paul and Kristin and quietly said, "Lack of trust is driven by perfectionism, and leads to hoarding ministry." David slid back into his chair. All three sat there finishing their meal. The only sound was the occasional clank of a metal utensil on the china.

Paul broke the silence with a softly worded question. "What do you mean by hoarding ministry?"

David looked straight at Paul. "When only the pastor calls on hospitalized members, it deprives members of sharing and growing their faith. If the pastor is the only one who makes ministry calls on shut-ins, it deprives the shut-ins of being ministered to frequently by members and it deprives the members of experiencing spiritual growth. When the pastor or a handful of other people need to agree with all decisions, the ministry growth of the majority of the members is stymied."

> ## Hoarding ministry stunts spiritual growth.

David concluded by asserting, "It may sound harsh, but when one or a few people dominate all activity and decision-making in congregations, they are hoarding the ministry and the ministry will eventually stagnate or die."

Paul tried to recover from the shock of what had just been said. He grasped the logic but was offended by the implication. He simply asserted, "You are making a rather rash judgment condemning a lot of people."

David replied, "Actually not. All of us who study congregations come to the same observations about the differences between struggling and thriving ministries. In struggling ministries there is a lot of what Ken Blanchard describes as EGOcentric ministry. Ken reminds us that EGO stands for Edging God Out."

> EGO means Edging God Out
> – Ken Blanchard

David continued. "In most thriving ministries there are high levels of trust, with many people making decisions, and the senior leadership or the pastor is only directly involved in the biggest decisions. They recognize that as important as Bible study is, Bible study is not ministry. Bible study prepares people for ministry. A lot of people like to think of committee meetings as ministry, but they are not ministry. Some committee meetings prepare for the delivery of ministry. Jesus didn't say 'Go ye therefore and hold meetings.' Jesus said, 'Go ye therefore and make disciples.'"

Kristin had been quiet for a long time. She knew that Paul needed to hear this, but she also knew how hard it would be for him.

To her amazement, David turned to Kristin and said, "We find that so often the pastor's spouse is generally aware that the ministry is in trouble. Sometimes the spouse sees characteristics in the pastor that make the ministry harder than it needs to be. As we listened to spouses and children of clergy, our hearts were glad for the love they displayed, but sad that they felt trapped. They know how hard the pastor works and don't want to add to the burden. They become ensnared in a real-life Catch-22 of seeing problems but not wanting to raise the issue and create more problems. Some just check out of the situation and focus their attention elsewhere."

Kristin shivered. So far she had only spent a short time with David, and yet he seemed to know what she was thinking. She also thought about how she had retreated into her world at work to escape. She knew that she needed the escape to maintain some balance in life, but she didn't feel good about leaving her husband alone more often. She quietly muttered, "At least it's out in the open now."

The dinner had been consumed. Actually, it was more picked at under the weight of discussing significant and life-changing issues. The table was being cleared and the server asked about dessert. Nobody was hungry.

Paul gave the server his credit card. Then he broke the silence by asking, "What can I do with my congregation when I get back."

David offered, "I'd encourage you to split that into two parts. The first part has to do with you and the second part has to do with the congregation. We can talk about what might be done with the congregation at a later time. As I said earlier, you have accomplished a major first task by recognizing that there is a problem. This weekend you have also crossed a major hurdle by asking for help. The third step on the road to recovery is to come to grips with your own ability to trust members and manage your perfectionism."

Paul asked, "How would you suggest I do that?"

David answered, but indirectly at first. "Many judicatories have someone who can help pastors in this kind of situation. Sometimes it is a counselor or therapist, sometimes a toll-free help line, and sometimes the judicatory leader."

Paul thought about the "help" he had previously received from the judicatory leader. He wondered what would happen to his career if the judicatory leader had to step in for this second congregation problem in a row.

David made Paul's thought stream more difficult by asking, "Does your judicatory or denomination have someone who can help?"

Paul had mixed emotions about whether the judicatory could actually be helpful and the fallout that might result if he went to them. So he just muttered, "I think so."

David had heard this kind of uncertainty many times from other pastors. He suggested, "One possibility is for you to contact that person and have a general discussion. See how you react and whether you feel you can build trust. If the discussion is going well, then just ask straight out about who is informed and what information is provided to others."

Paul was considering the suggestion, but he was still unsure. David decided to offer another possibility. "There are two other places to look. Some denominations have a medical insurance program with a toll-free number for counseling. Another source of help used by many pastors is to develop a friendship with a nearby pastor, often from a different denomination. That helps preserve confidentiality so important to being helped."

David decided to elaborate. "The suggestion to find someone to whom you can talk has a deeper value than simply a place to vent frustrations or test out ideas. The more important value is the opportunity to privately and confidentially offer confession and receive absolution. Many pastors preach and teach grace and forgiveness. Yet they are so absorbed in themselves and getting their way that they lose sight of the need for personal repentance. Strength of ministry comes from the power of Christ, not the power of personal performance. You will find great peace if you can come to rely on Christ rather than on yourself. Having a person to whom you can make your confession is a tremendous asset for you, your family, and your ministry."

Paul thought for a minute, then offered, "We do have a ministry alliance in our community. I have a growing relationship with a pastor whose congregation seems to be flourishing."

David encouraged Paul to consider that option. Then David continued. "Yesterday and this morning I had the impression there are a number of issues festering at your congregation. Without going into detail, is that right?"

Paul simply said, "Yes."

David went on. "You might consider going to one or two of the senior leadership groups to thank them and the congregation for giving you one Sunday off. We both know that you should have more, but leave that alone for now. Second, tell them you are aware that there has been some tension around new programs or ideas and you think it might be good to suspend work on them for a few months. Those opposed to the ideas will like the stoppage. But be sure to use the word 'suspend' so that the people in favor of the ideas will not feel betrayed.

"Tell the leaders it will be healthy for you to spend the next several months visiting every household in the congregation, and ask the leaders to support you in that activity. Point out to them that this important activity will mean you are not able to attend very many evening or weekend activities. Explain that you are confident they will carry on well during your temporary absence from the meetings."

Kristin smiled and observed, "That's a pretty interesting idea. Suspending discussions that lead to conflict will reduce tension in the church. Everyone will receive a personal contact from the pastor. The committees might find they don't need Paul to make decisions."

David looked at Paul and agreed that, "Kristin's observations are correct." As he spoke, Kristin noticed that David seemed to be holding something back. She was pleased to have her observation affirmed, but wanted to know what David was reluctant to say. She decided to simply ask, "David, what else do you want to say?"

David's serious expression helped Paul brace himself as David replied, "There is a third message you might think about giving to the leadership groups. But don't give it unless you are serious. The message is that you will also be looking for times when your actions have been offensive, so that you can ask for forgiveness."

David prepared for Paul's reaction. Paul sat back, deep in thought. Kristin held her breath. Finally Paul looked at David and said, "I don't know about that."

David was happy that Paul seemed at least willing to think about this third message. Most pastors either reject the notion of becoming vulnerable about their ministry, or they quickly agree, only to conduct a lip-service activity they do not take to heart.

David broke the ice with a relaxed suggestion. "Paul, for tonight let's just leave it that you will think about this idea of finding out about times when offense has been given. As you decide whether or not you can adopt this third message, you might want to remember your experience last night."

Paul had a quizzical expression, so David elaborated. "This morning you described the joy of grace you experienced last night by confessing that you had wronged your family, asked for, and received forgiveness. Remember how hard that was, but how much of a load was lifted afterward?"

David was not really expecting to hear an answer. He could see Paul's mood lighten as he recalled the wonder of grace and forgiveness. David finished his thought by saying, "That same feeling of relief and invigoration is waiting for you with the congregation's leaders and members."

David waited a bit to allow Paul time to absorb the notion that the obsession with ministry activity that had caused family problems might also apply within the congregation. Kristin was also silent.

Finally, Paul simply said, "It makes me uncomfortable, but I'll think about it."

David affirmed Paul by simply saying "great."

With a softer tone David leaned forward and continued. "There is another reason for doing this visitation. Ask the members what they enjoy doing in life, not limited to work or church. Ask them to talk about their passions."

At that point a memory popped into David's head. His eyes twinkled as he asked, "Do you remember that earlier I mentioned my mentor, Kennon Callahan?"

"Yes. In fact I have heard of him before."

"Kennon has a wonderful way of describing this process as being more invitational than inquisitive. He has a delightful invitation that goes like this, 'Share with me where you were born and what has happened since.'"

Paul had a puzzled look, but Kristin's eyes sparkled as she remarked, "What a delightful invitation. You get to hear what is important to them by what they talk about and don't talk about, by the emotions they display or don't display, and how animated they are."

David smiled as he again realized what a strong team these two could be in ministry. "Two things will happen when you offer this type of invitation. First, you will learn to be a better listener. Second, you will discover the many gifts God has given to the congregation. You will hear dozens of stories about gifts, strengths, competencies, hopes, fears, dreams, and aspirations. You will discover that most of the gifts God has blessedly given the congregation have been untapped or don't fit within the congregation's organization chart, constitution, or by-laws."

"As you arrange for these visits, be open to where they can take place. Some people will be eager to have you visit them at work, where they attend school, at recreational events, and so on. You will get to know them better because they will be in what for them is a relaxing location. Feel free to start with families who attend worship regularly. I'd invite you to include those who participate with the congregation but are not members. In fact, you might even find you enjoy the opportunity to meet people from the community as you make these visits."

David concluded with the most important part of the visitation suggestion. "Practice seeing yourself as a person who helps people find their way into ministry. Not attending meetings about ministry, but ministry itself. As you do, make mental notes about places where you will need to trust the members and reduce your tendency toward perfectionism. What you will be doing is increasing your shepherding skills. Kristin will help you. God will help you. This isn't self-help. Self-help is lonely and rarely makes more than a temporary difference. Pray to God for help and thank God for giving you Kristin and the congregation's members. Give me a call when you and Kristin agree that you have made excellent progress. Don't look for perfection. As Kennon is so fond of reminding people, 'Progress is more helpful than perfection.'"

> Progress is more helpful than perfection.
> – Kennon Callahan

As David looked upon these two wonderful people, he could see that they were exhausted. With a soft tone, he said, "I can see that you both are about ready for a good night of rest."

Paul and Kristin looked at each other and realized how tired they were.

Even though there was more that could have been said, David decided to conclude with one point that is critical when pastors take a "time out" from their normal ministry activities. "As you make these visits, remember that the committees are used to your being there all the time. At first they will be reluctant to make decisions without you. You will do well to encourage them by saying things like, 'I'm sure you can make an excellent decision about that' rather than making the decision yourself. They will ask for your opinion. When they do, your first thought should not be about your opinion. Your first thought should be to ask yourself if you should even give your opinion at all. Most all the time, you should not."

> First ask yourself,
>   "Should I even answer this question?"

David touched Paul's arm, saying, "Paul, this will be very hard for you." Then David looked at Kristin but spoke to Paul, "You have the tremendous blessing that Kristin will help you." David looked back at Paul. "Review with Kristin every one of these incidents as they come up over the next few weeks and together decide if they were handled appropriately. It will help you learn a new behavior."

Paul looked over at Kristin. Kristin was beaming as they exchanged unspoken words of mutual love and support.

Paul reached out one hand to Kristin and the other hand to David. David and Kristin completed the circle as Paul closed his eyes to say, "Thank you God. The many odd accidents of yesterday make it clear that your hand has been guiding these two days. I recognize that I need help and rededicate myself to your call to me. Thank you for my wonderful wife, our children, and for our new friend. Thank you for the reminder of the power repentance and forgiveness and the firsthand experience with grace. Please give me strength and wisdom to learn what I'm beginning to see I need. I'm so grateful to you Oh God for your guidance, your strength, and for salvation through Jesus Christ. Amen."

CHAPTER 8

Missionary/Shepherd

The two friends chatted by phone every week or two over the ensuing three months. Paul described initial skepticism from the congregation's leaders. They finally went along with his idea since the church year was winding down after Easter anyway.

David helped Paul stay focused on the two primary reasons for the visits with members. Paul often needed reminders not to disagree or correct members during his time with them. Eventually Paul came to understand that timing is important. By truly listening in the early visits, Paul learned that being able to give help requires that the listener is ready to receive help at the time it is offered.

At the same time, Paul began to understand what David meant by a compulsion toward perfectionism. Paul came to see that even though his members dealt with their lives in ways that would not have been Paul's first choice, most seemed to be coping with life just fine.

Paul's attention to the second reason for the visits proved extremely enlightening. He discovered an almost unbelievable collection of skills and passions possessed by the congregation's members. Some could be useful in the congregation's current structure, but the majority just did not fit. Paul uncovered a long list of ways people could be involved in mission if only the church had a way to use those energies.

The midsummer day when David and Paul met was comfortable and sunny. They decided to move their discussion out from David's office to the lake at a nearby park. The sky and water were as blue as the day they met. Green grass and trees framed views toward the infinite horizon in one direction and mountain peaks in the other. It was a glorious day.

Paul began by saying, "Kristin and I want to thank you for helping our family reconnect. We are spending more time together doing things we like to do. I'm not so distracted by details at church as I once was. We even decided to use the answering machine to screen telephone calls that come at dinner or during family time. I was amazed to discover that less than one in ten of those calls truly needed immediate attention."

David replied with a simple, "That's great."

"Also," Paul continued, "things are calmer around church. I'm not so intense and the members seem to have relaxed. Perhaps it is just the nice summer days."

David injected, "People lead the way they experience being led."

Paul smiled and admitted, "I used to blame all my problems with congregation members and leaders on them. I'm beginning to see that many stem from me and my predecessor. Both of us strove to be perfect rather than relying to God. Neither of us trusted anyone other than ourselves."

Paul then reminded David, "You said we could discuss several congregation level issues after I dealt with my personal issues."

"Right. It seems to me that you have started to recognize tendencies toward perfectionism. You have also begun to see ministry potential in your members and not just see them as a means to fill slots on committees. Those two are big hurdles. Without recognizing both, you will never be able to grasp the larger congregation issues."

Paul was eager to hear more, so he just said, "Okay."

David continued. "Paul, why did you want to be a parish pastor?"

Paul quickly replied to this easy question. "To help people."

David stunned Paul by saying, "Even an atheist can want to help people."

David did not need to continue the thought. Paul knew exactly the point. And yet, for all his preparation to be a pastor, he had never spent any time confronting this basic point. Rather than admit discomfort, Paul responded, "I also felt a calling from God to serve people."

David did not back off from this key issue. He asked, "What did Jesus specifically call you and others to do?"

Two thoughts simultaneously came to Paul's mind. He replied, "To be a shepherd to His flock and to make disciples."

As soon as the words passed Paul's lips he remembered David's comments about shepherd and sheep. David gave him a knowing smile and Paul smiled back, saying, "I was pretty upset with your comments about sheep, how sheep might feel about shepherds and how shepherds feel about their sheep. I suspect you have more to suggest on that topic."

David was glad Paul was willing to listen to more thoughts about shepherds and sheep. Most pastors hearing David's analysis would have become highly offended and simply stopped listening.

David was relaxed as he explained, "Pastors often use Jesus' statement to be a shepherd to their flock in discussions about the outreach record of their congregation. Rather, I should say, the lack of outreach record of their congregation. Most congregations confirm or baptize relatively few adults each year. We celebrate each one, but at the same time recognize that perhaps half of the few that come to faith do so because of marriage or other family issues."

David realized he was getting off the point, so he started over. "Many pastors seem to use their calling to be a shepherd as a definition of their ministry focus on the needs of current members, and only pay lip service to the masses of effectively unchurched people in the local mission field on which God has placed them. We were curious about and decided to investigate how Jesus conducted his ministry on this point of shepherd or missionary."

Paul was fascinated and asked, "How did you do that?"

David explained, "The Book of Matthew has a helpful literary style. Before each group of passages, Matthew describes who is talking, who is listening, and a bit about the context. We were able to count the number of verses in which Jesus is focused on the faithful followers, church officials, or people in the mission field. We excluded verses that were historical descriptions."

David observed that Paul was eagerly listening, so he continued. "We made two helpful discoveries. First, we found that Matthew recorded Jesus spending almost as much time in the mission field as he spent addressing his faithful followers. Second, the early chapters of Matthew report Jesus primarily in the mission field and in the later chapters Jesus spent more time with the faithful followers."

Paul added, "So in the early chapters Jesus demonstrated outreach. Then, in the later chapters He helped the faithful followers to get ready for handling the Great Commission."

David was pleased that Paul grasped the analogy. He cautioned, "Of course, there probably are some technical objections to this analysis, but the overall point is clear about Jesus' personal ministry and His message to us. Making disciples is a critical element of ministry. Disciples may attend meetings and classes, but the purpose is so that those same disciples can function as missionaries. Being a missionary was certainly as important to Jesus as was tending to the flock."

Paul was puzzled and asked, "That certainly is interesting, but what is the point?"

David returned to the earlier question about why people enter ministry by asking Paul, "You have to ask yourself a very serious question. The question concerns the relative importance of the Great Commission to your personal ministry."

Paul caught on and asked the question of himself, "What is my level of commitment to and responsibility for achieving the Great Commission?"

David went on. "You see, during the days of the churched society, up through about 1970 or so, it was the 'thing to do' to go to church. During those days churched people thought of the Great Commission in terms of foreign continents or social services to their community's less fortunate people. In current times, at least half of every community is effectively unchurched. Rural communities, often described as highly churched places, are generally at least fifty percent unchurched. The numbers get worse as population density increases. In larger cities, the population of unchurched runs as high as eighty and ninety percent."

Paul quietly replied, "Wow."

David continued. "We came to understand the importance of the focus on ministry questions from two separate types of findings. During interviews we heard pastors of stagnant or dying churches vigorously refer to themselves as shepherds of the flock. In contrast, pastors of congregations effectively reaching unchurched people never use the shepherd metaphor. They describe their work in terms used by missionaries. They talk about learning the local language and then discovering how to communicate in that language. They are adamant about preserving their theological stance, while open to learning new ways of communicating those unchanging truths.

Great Commission pastors:
1. Learn the mission field's language.
2. Learn how to communicate in that language.
3. Keep theological truths while learning new ways to communicate those truths.

"The second way that the focus of ministry clearly surfaced came in comparing struggling congregations with thriving ministries. Struggling congregations focus all their attention and effort on themselves. They are inwardly focused. They say that anyone is welcome to join, but do very little or nothing to ease the way in for outsiders. Thriving ministries focus their attention on reaching lost people with the saving message of Jesus. They see themselves as a mission outpost on a mission field. They see their congregation as reaching out to broken and hurting people with a healing Jesus."

Paul jumped in by asserting that, "Both of the congregations I have served included outreach as important parts of their mission statement and constitution."

David interrupted to point out, "Yes, constitutions and mission statements usually include outreach. However, we find it more helpful to analyze the monthly calendar of activities and the minutes of the senior lay leadership group meetings."

Paul asked, "How do you assess those?"

David explained, "We put the letter S by every activity listed on the calendar that supports the structure of the congregation. Activities like elders meetings, choir, finance committee, and the like. We put the letter M by those activities specifically for or primarily attended by the members, such as classes, circles, dinners, and so forth. Finally, we put the letter N by activities specifically designed for nonmembers. The resulting tabulation provides a picture of the actual mission of the congregation."

> Monthly activity calendar classifications:
> S = Structure
> M = Members
> N = Nonmembers

Paul was silent as he pictured in his mind the calendar he had just completed for the next month. David was hitting pretty close to home.

David continued. "We also tabulate how much time is spent in the senior lay leadership group meetings on which topics. We use the same three classifications. How congregations spend their corporate time, as displayed on the calendar, and how they spend their leadership time, as listed in the meeting minutes, defines the actual mission of the congregation."

Paul quietly reflected on this insight. He could see the implications. He had to admit that neither of his congregations had been seriously pursuing the Great Commission.

He was also reflecting on what this meant for him personally when David touched him on the arm and said, "Let me tell you what this all has meant for your ministry experience in the two congregations."

Paul had gotten used to David knowing what was going on in his mind. It was clear that David had been through this type of discussion many times before. Paul decided to continue listening rather than getting mad and storming off.

David leaned forward and said, "Inwardly focused congregations have many issues. They are so self-centered that the congregations and the people within the congregations focus on themselves. The members push and shove on each other to get their way. They run off any pastor who disagrees with them. If the pastor refuses to leave, some members leave while others stay to continue the fight until the pastor eventually dies or leaves."

Paul was not able to admit that he was run out of his first congregation, but he did recall the disappearance of his confirmation pastor so long ago.

David hit home when he said, "Individuals in congregations who are not able to get their way will accuse pastors of failing to do their duties. They will complain about pastors not visiting the sick fast enough and ignore the impossibility of that demand when the pastor isn't notified or can't get there quickly. They will let the building maintenance deteriorate, knowing full well that the pastor's perfectionism will force the pastor to do the custodial work. They will punish the pastor by providing a wage so small it only permits the basics of life. They will make it clear that prior pastors had not measured up and that the current pastor will face a similar fate for not toeing the line."

Suddenly, Paul understood what happened at his first congregation. David could see the light bulb go on in Paul's eyes, so he stopped to give Paul time to soak up the critical concept.

After several minutes Paul said, "Now I understand what was going on in my first congregation. I guess that on some subconscious level I knew that when I decided to take firm control in my current congregation."

David spoiled Paul's sense of satisfaction by asserting, "Yes, and the same problem exists in your second congregation, except that now the pastor is doing the pushing around rather than being pushed around by the members."

Paul was stunned by this assertion, but David continued, "Both of your congregational experiences are marked by what Ken Blanchard calls EGOcentric behavior. Sometimes members, sometimes pastors, but often both, are so focused on getting their way that God gets edged out. Remember Blanchard's reminder that EGO stands for Edging God Out."

Paul was crushed by this assertion. He wanted to object, but he knew the importance of continuing to listen and arguing later. He simply said, "I've got my pencil sharpened, so please continue."

Both men smiled at Paul's little joke.

David relaxed his body in hopes that Paul would relax. David said, "There is good news. We never find pushing and shoving in Great Commission-focused congregations. Great Commission congregations are simply too busy being a mission outpost in their local mission field to waste time on EGO. These congregations do have problems and the people don't always agree with each other. However, all differences of opinion are framed within the overall Great Commission ministry of the congregation. Differences of opinion are used to strengthen ideas rather than excuses for a fight to the death. Levels of trust are so high in Great Commission congregations that those who might disagree with this or that decision spend their energy helping to make the chosen course of action work. They are not involved in destructive gossip or plotting the downfall of other members or the pastor."

David paused for effect and then added, "Great Commission congregations are focused on reaching the lost—just like the Good Shepherd leaving the flock behind to locate the one lost sheep."

Paul's mind was spinning. This had been a lot to take, even on such a lovely day. His mind raced through past fights and disputes at his current congregation. He began to see a flood of realities that matched what David described. He said, "I can see how these insights are helpful to improving the atmosphere in congregations."

David redirected Paul's thoughts by saying, "Let's get together in a month to talk about the implications for congregations."

Paul was a bit thrown. He wanted to talk about his congregation.

David quickly explained. "Before addressing congregation issues, pastors have to be clear about their view of ministry. It is very easy to become consumed by functional details of congregations. Paul, you need to carefully think through your personal direction as a parish pastor. You have to search your soul to discover how you see ministry. If you want to be a shepherd absorbed by the needs of the flock, you can do that. If you are truly committed to being a Great Commission pastor, you can do that."

Paul objected, saying, "I want to do both."

David had heard this assertion many times, always by pastors leading inwardly focused congregations. He hoped Paul would bear with him for just a little longer. "Yes, it is possible to do both, but not in the way you currently understand. Let me show you exactly what I mean. Do you have your personal planner?"

Paul said yes and pulled it out.

David said "great" as he produced a note pad and pencil.

David continued. "Open your planner to three months ago while I make three columns on this sheet of paper. Column S is for the time spent on structure, column M is for members, and column N is for nonmembers."

Paul turned to February and held the planner so both could see.

David pointed to February 1 and said, "We will place a tick mark for every hour of activity under the corresponding column. The first entry is a seven in the morning meeting for two hours. What do you talk about in those meetings?"

Paul explained it was for coordination of activity details. David replied, "Fine. That's two tick marks under the S column. Eleven o'clock says Dorcas Circle. I assume that's a group of mostly older women doing service projects for the congregation."

With a startled look Paul asked, "How did you know that?"

David simply smiled and put one tick mark under the M column as an activity for members.

Paul objected. "Nonmembers can participate."

David asked, "How often do they attend?"

Paul thought for a minute and then admitted, "Not very often."

David pointed to the ten to noon slot notation "sermon preparation." David asked, "How should we classify your sermons?"

Paul said, "I'd like to think they are helpful to both members and nonmembers."

David offered, "Let me help you with two questions. First, as you prepare sermons are you specifically thinking about unchurched people who are biblically illiterate?"

Paul said, "Well, no. But are you suggesting I should preach beginner sermons to long-term members?"

David answered, "Certainly not. But we'll get to that issue later. At this point we simply want to tabulate how you spend your time. It is important for you to examine in a realistic way the degree to which your ministry has balance so you can compare your behavior with your philosophies of ministry.

"For now, please trust me that what I would like you to do next will be helpful. Please try to make what might seem to be an unnecessary choice. If you had to choose between being a shepherd taking care of basically unruly sheep and a missionary on your congregation's local mission field, which would you choose?"

Paul was feeling drained. He noticed that he always felt tired after discussions with David. However, Paul also felt his strength for ministry returning.

The two men checked their calendars and agreed to meet at the same time and place the next month.

Before parting, David made a suggestion. "This is not an easy decision. You might want to search the scriptures and take these matters to our Lord in prayer. Discuss it with Kristin. The answer will define the remainder of your ministry."

CHAPTER 9

Shared Ministry

One month to the day later, David and Paul again met by the lake in the park. Fleecy clouds floated across the sky, the kind that children and dreamers transform into objects.

Paul seemed subdued as they greeted each other with pleasantries about family and the weather. Paul seemed a bit troubled and was eager to start. It had not been an easy month, mostly because he could not agree with David's request that Paul choose between being a shepherd or a missionary. The scripture that came to Paul seemed dominated by the ministry of his namesake, Paul the Apostle. Pastor Paul found himself haunted by the story of Apostle Paul in Athens finding a way to communicate in terms that the people of that city could understand.

He explained his dilemma by saying, "The choice you asked me to make was a tough one. I'm not sure I accept the premise. But, if I have to choose between focusing inward or outward, I feel more drawn to the Great Commission part of that choice. I can't exactly say why, but if forced to choose, that is where I would go."

David accepted the partial decision, knowing that the explanation he was about to provide would clarify the validity of the question's forced choice.

David began with an apology. "Paul, I am sorry for having put you through a difficult time with what seems like an unnecessary choice. Here is why. Decades of listening to congregations and pastors who say they want to be both inwardly and outwardly focused has shown that when pastors or congregations have to make a specific choice about programs, activities, or money, they always choose to meet the needs of current members. What actually happens is that members come to insist on their point of view. Little issues become big power struggles. Positions harden and the atmosphere in the congregation deteriorates. Someone eventually has to leave and often it's the pastor."

"Some seemingly inwardly focused congregations are surviving."

David accepted Paul's observation by saying, "The term surviving is correct. Most of these congregations cruise through their year-in and year-out patterns with very little outreach results. They appear to thrive, but only while their community is expanding. When no more new houses are built or the community changes, the congregations start to stagnate or deteriorate. Sometimes a forceful pastor leaves and the congregation's pent-up hostility overwhelms the next pastor. Virtually all congregations primarily focused on taking care of their current members can be characterized in one of two ways. Either they are stagnant or declining, or they are already small and barely surviving."

David emphasized, "Some congregations are dominated by the will of their pastor. They appear to be stable. However, looking at their numbers reveals that they grow only to the point that their dominant ministry leader can control everything. One individual can direct only a fixed number of details. When that limit is reached, the congregation will only replace the members who leave. Some see this and use the word 'stable,' but others see the congregation as being 'stagnant.' Whatever term is used, the number of effectively unchurched people on the local mission field who find their way into that congregation each year is very limited."

In his mind, Paul ticked through the congregations in his area. He had to admit that this characterization was sadly accurate.

David continued. "In contrast, outwardly focused congregations *never* have to make the choice I asked you to make. They realize that the best way to meet the needs of members is to focus on their spiritual growth. They understand that spiritual growth happens best in missional activity, not in meetings. Bible study is important in Great Commission congregations, but it's a way of preparing for the actual delivery of mission and not just for intellectual stimulation. Remember that John 3:16 says 'For God so loved the world that he gave his only begotten son.' It does not say 'For God so loved *the church*.'"

David paused and Paul simply said, "Go on."

David drew close to Paul and said, "I'll let you in on a little secret. Before we interview groups of pastors, we examine the pattern of average weekly worship attendance over the past ten years at their congregation."

David's voice became softer. "In our latest study we estimated that about one in five pastors are experiencing severe professional burnout and a like number are rapidly approaching severe burnout. Burnout does not mean, 'I need a vacation.' Burnout means, 'I'd quit this job tomorrow if it wouldn't screw up my pension.'"

David went on. "Our clearest and most powerful finding is that almost all the burned out pastors are in congregations experiencing declining average weekly worship attendance."

Paul was stunned. And yet he had to admit to himself that this description matched his situation. Sadly, Paul also admitted to himself that it matched other pastors he suspected of being in trouble.

David waited a while before continuing. The sun was warm and the light breeze felt good.

Finally Paul said, "I'm sensing that all these points are connected."

David smiled. "Everything we have talked about since we first met on the gondola is connected. The central concept can be approached from any starting point. So, I'll start with your sleepless nights."

Paul was taken aback. In all their time together, Paul had never mentioned that he often had trouble falling asleep or only slept for a few hours before experiencing insomnia.

"How did you know?"

David replied, "I have good news for you. First, you are not alone. And second, there is a way out."

David then leaned back and said, "Let's review. You have been able to admit and confess that you are struggling and your ministry is in trouble. You have been able to ask for help and been willing to be helped. You have been comforted in the good news that God forgives. You have examined your own understanding of ministry and found that if forced to make a choice, you would like to focus on our Lord's Great Commission."

Paul was heartened by this summary of progress. He smiled broadly and proudly exclaimed, "Right!"

David smiled back at Paul and then turned serious. "You are now ready to consider the way out of your ministry despair and into ministry health. It is important that pastors and congregations have a common understanding of the purpose of the congregation. This may seem an obvious statement, but all too often it is ignored. We found that over half of all clergy firings resulted from a mismatch between the congregation's and pastor's understanding of ministry."

Paul was listening intently, so David continued. "When congregations focus on the Great Commission, they are also focusing on building the spirituality of their members. These congregations aggressively find ways to help members discover ministries that directly touch the lives of people. They are not consumed by large amounts of time in meetings. The congregations remove barriers to new ideas and embrace of sense a trusting each other in the work of the Lord."

Paul injected, "That sounds wonderful."

David came right back, not giving Paul a chance to comment further. "There is more. Great Commission congregations are marked by action, not meetings. They have a spirit of cooperation, not conflict. Members are active in using their particular gifts and passions directly in ministry. The terms 'lay mobilization' or 'ministry mobilization' are used these days to describe this passion of connecting people with ministry. It isn't slot filling, designed to solve the problems of the nominations committee. Involving people in ministry helps them grow spiritually. The whole situation feeds and nourishes itself. It is truly a marvel to behold."

David paused for a couple of minutes to allow Paul the opportunity to soak up this picture. Then he touched Paul on the arm and said, "When we met in the gondola, you were feeling depressed about your ministry. You feel better now, but that is primarily because you and the congregation have declared a temporary truce over the summer. With fall approaching, the church year's activities are about to start and soon you will be looking at next year's budget."

Paul simply nodded and quietly said, "Yep." He was remembering the tug of wills that he went through developing last year's budget.

David kept going. "Remember that people lead the way they experience being led. When the pastor is focused on details, the members will focus on details. Members, leaders, and pastors focusing on details provide hundreds of opportunities every month for disagreement, differences of opinion, and fighting. Pastors that focus on the Great Commission become effective leaders of congregation members focused on the Great Commission. Most operational decisions made in congregations can be made by one or two people. This does not mean the same one or two people handle all decisions. It means that most functional detail decisions are made by the one or two people with the best competence to handle the decision. When the pastor's tendency toward perfectionism drives the need for involvement in all decisions, the members learn not to trust each other or the pastor. Pastors set the tone."

> ## Pastoral perfectionism breeds low levels of trust.

Paul inserted, "Yes, but they get mad if I am not involved in all the meetings."

David countered, "That is because they are focused internally and on control. When they become committed to the Great Commission, everything changes. Great Commission-dominated congregations simply don't have time for internal turmoil. I'll bet that your congregation's senior lay leadership meetings are a miscellaneous series of reports on unrelated activities."

Paul agreed, "Yes, I suppose so."

David explained, "Senior lay leadership meetings at Great Commission-focused congregations spend the majority of their time looking at the big picture of the congregation's overall ministry. They only handle the relatively few major decisions assigned to them by the congregation. They have problems. Sometimes they have big problems. Overall, they focus on ways the congregation can continue to improve its effectiveness in achieving the congregation's overall ministry."

David became more animated as he observed, "And you know what? Ministry becomes fun. It becomes fun for the pastor and the members. It isn't hard work, in the sense of bearing down or struggle. Struggling pastors and congregations often say they simply need to work harder and things will get better. The opposite is the case. You see, when people work harder, they just get more tired. As they become more tired, they tend to also become more grumpy. Grumpy people create tension and mistrust, causing the ministry to struggle. Thriving ministries are filled with joy."

Paul was beginning to catch David's enthusiasm. "That sounds great."

David kept going. "Here's the best part. Great Commission congregations never have to choose between taking care of their members and reaching out to others. By focusing on the Great Commission, they meet the needs of their current members in the most remarkable ways. Sadly, inwardly directed congregations never seem able to satisfy members. Why? Because you can never fully satisfy a self-centered person."

> **You can never satisfy a self-centered person.**

Paul remembered the choice David had asked him to make. Once again, David seemed to know what Paul was thinking.

David leaned back and quieted his voice. "Some people describe the Great Commission as a stern command to GO." David's sharp tone on the word "go" startled Paul.

Quietly David continued, "I'm not sure that is the most helpful view. I like Kennon Callahan's suggestion that the Great Commission is more of an invitation."

David looked directly at Paul and asked, "Do you remember that famous painting of Jesus knocking at the door?"

Paul answered, "Of course. Jesus is knocking at the door of our hearts asking to be allowed in."

David nodded and said, "Yes, that's it. Kennon helped me see that painting in a new light. Now when I see it, I think of my boyhood chum knocking on our front door and yelling 'can David come out and play?' I now think of that painting as Jesus knocking at the door of our church asking us to come out into the mission field on which we are located."

> Jesus is knocking at the door of our hearts, inviting us out into the mission field.

David looked straight at Paul and said, "My friend, this is the path out of ministry depression and despair. The way forward is found by focusing on Christ and our forgiveness, which in turn compels us into our local mission field. This refocus of ministry starts within ourselves and extends into the congregation with a matching direction."

Paul reflected on David's words. They made sense. But, more than making sense, they seemed to be a way out of the constant tension and turmoil that marked so many of the meetings and were causing sleepless nights.

Paul asked, "How do I proceed?"

David was happy for Paul. He knew that Paul's life was about to get better. He knew that Paul's ministry was about to become more meaningful to Paul and to the congregation. At the same time, David realized that change of focus does not happen overnight, and that some would resist as their ability to hold the congregation hostage to their own views might be challenged.

David leaned back, putting his arm across the bench's backrest, and began, "As I have been saying since our dinner at the Charthouse, you have made an excellent start. The next step for you is to learn about being a missionary pastor who leads a Great Commission congregation. You will have to learn about the change from the churched society of decades and centuries ago into the unchurched society of current times. I will send you some books that will help."

Paul inserted, "Great!"

David continued, "You will also find it helpful to learn from some pastors who have created Great Commission congregations. I will send you a few of their books and a listing of their conferences. As you read or listen, remember these pastors all started with small congregations that became large because they became highly skilled at reaching unchurched people, helping them come to faith, and nourishing spiritual growth. As you read or listen, remember that size and growth are not the issues. The issue is focus of ministry."

The issue is focus of ministry.

Paul volunteered, "I'll be sure to remember that."

David went on. "While you are learning, you will find yourself beginning to form your own vision of Great Commission ministry. You will find one of the models of ministry more comfortable than the others. I'd suggest that you pick one and emulate it, rather than flitting from one to another or spending a lot of time creating a customized approach to something you will not fully grasp until a few years from now."

Paul added, "That makes sense. But what about my congregation?"

David was pleased to hear Paul recognizing that the pastor and the congregation are not one and the same. Just because the pastor adopts some particular point of view does not mean the congregation will go along. Sometimes they openly object, and other times they say nothing until the meeting in which the pastor is asked to resign.

David held up his index finger as he exclaimed, "Excellent point. Many pastors make the mistake of failing to accept that changing from inward focus to mission outreach can be difficult—especially as some individuals begin to realize they will no longer be allowed to dominate. A fascinating fact is that a few individuals dominate congregations primarily because congregation members don't want to endure the pain of objecting."

Realizing that he was straying from the point, David took a breath and went on. "The key issue for you is to help your congregation learn along with you. If you keep in mind that people lead the way they experience being led, you will begin to see a host of ways to help the congregation grow into a Great Commission focus. This Great Commission focus comes from within the Word, not from within yourself. It is a response to the invitation of Christ to 'Go and make disciples,' and not from a new obsession for numbers, size, or growth."

Paul asked, "Could you give me some examples?"

David responded, "Sure. Pay attention to your words at meetings, in newsletters, and especially in sermons. Look for opportunities to explain the changed culture and to describe outreach-oriented congregations."

Paul injected, "Good point."

David explained, "The most helpful way to grow forward as a mission outpost is to be in the mission field. A helpful place to start is with your appointment book. If the pastor is not active in the mission field, it is not reasonable to expect members to be active in the mission field."

> If the pastor is not active in the mission field,
> it is not reasonable to expect members to
> be active in the mission field.

David suggested, "Let's turn in your planner to next month." Paul flipped the pages to next month as David continued. "In February you only averaged five hours a week with nonmembers. Let's pick a total of fifteen hours each week next month."

With a confused tone, Paul asked, "Doing what?"

David smiled and replied, "For today, the specifics don't matter. What is important for now is to reserve the time so that structural and member issues don't crowd out time with nonmembers. The books I am sending you will provide hundreds of ideas on the specifics. Some of them are to visit with new people moving into the community, families living near the church, places where your members work, or local civic groups. You might attend intervention program groups led by or participated in by your members."

Paul reflected, "Yes, I found out about a lot of those when I visited the members."

David was glad at being able to comment, "It's great to see that you are catching on. Some in the congregation will object to not seeing your car at the church or not reaching you instantly when they call. Try to view their objection not as a challenge, but as an opportunity to spend some time getting to know that member's passions. Invite them to accompany you on these visits and then talk about what happened. Seek gentle, guiding ways to help them discover the great joy of Great Commission ministry."

David paused to give Paul time to think about this novel method of working with challenging people. David added, "This will be hard for some people who are combative. A few will not accept this approach. Always remember that you are the pastor to the whole congregation, not just certain members."

Paul's face displayed a feeling of excitement. "I'm eager to give that a try."

David decided to wrap up the conversation with a brief glimpse of the next steps available to Paul in working with the congregation. He explained, "As you go through the next months, be sure to share with the congregation's leaders what you are reading, learning, and experiencing. It can be helpful to include them in some of the activities you find are helpful. That will help them build enthusiasm for the last step necessary before the first stages of becoming a Great Commission congregation."

Paul asked, "What is that last step?"

David smiled as he said, "I'm going to tell you another story."

Paul laughed, knowing that David was about to go off on a tangent that would eventually come back to the discussion in a helpful way.

"Some years ago we had the opportunity to gather sixty-three Great Commission congregations of all sizes in the same place. The purpose was to listen to their experience. One of the activities was for each congregation to draw on a large poster a timeline of the congregation's history."

David leaned toward Paul. "We learned that every one of those congregations had some precipitating event that changed the congregation. Some were positive, like an inspiring new worker, and some were negative, like an indiscretion. All these events had two things in common. First, they impacted the entire congregation. Second, they caused the congregation to change their fundamental understanding of ministry. We came to call these 'congregation ignitor events.'"

Paul nodded, repeating, "An ignitor event. It causes the congregation to catch on fire."

David confirmed, "Correct. An ignitor event that helps the congregation catch the spark for Great Commission ministry."

Paul asked, "How do we make that happen?"

David replied, "Some congregations create their own and others secure assistance from outsiders. I'll send you some materials and references you and the congregation's leaders can check out."

David lowered his voice as a means of emphasis. "Either way, it is very important that whatever you do involves the whole congregation. Great Commission ministry is best built by a grassroots process, not a top-down approach."

> Great Commission ministry is best built
> by a grassroots process.

Paul queried, "What do you mean?"

David elaborated. "Take the example of developing a long-range plan. Most congregations use the following approach. A long-range planning team is appointed and sometimes a consultant is brought in to help. The team and the consultant will collect a large amount of information, often including opinions from members. Then the consultant may write a 'prescription' for what the congregation needs, or the team will write a plan. The plan is then 'sold' to the senior leadership group and then 'sold' to the voters."

Paul winced as he remembered himself using the term "sold" to describe past efforts in his congregations to get things accepted.

David continued. "A small number of voters attend the meetings and approve the plan. The leaders mistakenly assume that the voters will participate in implementing the plan. About half of these plans are then put on the shelf and nothing happens."

David again leaned forward. Paul had come to understand that this body language meant David was about to deliver another key point.

David said, "What the few voters present at the meeting really meant was, 'We don't violently object. You go ahead and do the plan if you want.' Leadership's problem is failing to recognize that it's no longer 1950. In the heady days of the churched culture, the leaders simply told the congregation what was going to happen and most members eagerly cooperated. Those days are gone and the top-down decision making developed during that time no longer works."

Paul knew it was coming, but could not resist a friendly jab. With a smile, Paul asked, "So what is your point?"

David smiled back at his friend, saying, "The point is that you and the congregation leaders need to come to grips with finding ways to help the congregation see the value, beauty, and fun of being a Great Commission congregation. You need to involve the whole congregation in creating the plan, not simply approving what others have decided. When we do this work in congregations, we will not come if the congregation leaders will not commit to an attendance goal of twenty to forty percent of average weekly worship attendance participating in the ignitor event. I'd suggest that you look for approaches or consultants who work with the whole congregation. Our research has shown that to be the best way forward for the congregation."

David looked squarely at Paul for his concluding thought. "Above all, pay attention to what is going on inside yourself as you read, listen, and encourage. It is helpful to develop a spirit of warmth and invitation rather than a tone of commanding or scolding. People respond better to love than brute force. Ask Kristin and a very trusted church member to mentor you in achieving this important, helpful, and effective way of communicating."

David paused, looked at the sky, and repeated, as much for himself as for Paul, "A spirit of invitation."

David stopped. Both men sat for a while in silence. They felt good about their time together that day. They basked in the warmth of the sun and their growing friendship. They felt a kinship toward each other and savored the shared calling from God to help others find their path to salvation and spiritual growth. It had been another great day in the Lord.

CHAPTER 10

Epilogue

Over the ensuing two years, David and Paul had many conversations. Some included Kristin, and others just the two men. David was particularly pleased to watch this wonderful family grow closer together, even as the children began to leave home. Yes, there were ups and downs. Old habits die hard. As a family, they found that the little reminders they exchanged during their all-nighter in the condo, along with their exchanged repentance and forgiveness, gave them a solid foundation on which to rebuild what had almost been destroyed.

Paul's path to personal and ministry peace was a pleasure to behold. He read the books David suggested and attended several of the conferences. Paul took the advice to become directly involved in the congregation's local mission field. He visited newcomers to the community. He prepared a helpful and inspiring message and found welcome audiences at regular meetings of a dozen civic groups. He visited members at their places of work, and enjoyed meeting their coworkers before work, during coffee breaks, at lunch, and after work.

Paul came to understand shepherding in a healthy way. He discovered that listening and offering a word of encouragement was a welcome difference in his behavior and seemed to be appreciated by members and others alike. He found himself abandoning the concept of a shepherd as a manipulative and controlling herder.

Paul noticed an unexpected effect on his daily schedule. He anticipated many problems caused by spending more time in the mission field, but found the opposite was the case. Sermon preparation time was dramatically decreased as Paul spent more time directly with members and in the mission field. He found that focusing on the mission of the congregation freed him for needing to "ride herd" on hundreds of details.

Most importantly, Paul found himself more at peace with himself, his family, and his ministry. His daily Bible study was returning to the richness he remembered from seminary days. He felt himself coming closer to God and to God's calling to him. He spent more time with his family. He was amazed to notice his feeling closer even to his oldest son who had moved away from home.

Paul was intrigued by comments from members. Most seemed to notice that something was different. A few asked if Paul had changed his hairstyle. Several remarked that he seemed more at peace.

They were right. Paul developed a growing peace and calm. By spending time personally in the mission field, he discovered a building enthusiasm for the joy of Great Commission ministry. He did not simply substitute one obsession with another. Rather, he rediscovered the Grace that comes from relying on God instead of the power of one person's personality or will.

Paul found this transformation also helped him confront his tendency for perfectionism. He discovered that he could truly trust the members, and they in turn trusted him. The notion that "people lead the way they experience being led" was reflected in the congregation's transformation.

Paul's way forward was a blessing to him and to the congregation, but was not without objections. A few were disturbed when he stopped attending all board and committee meetings except the two key senior leadership groups. Paul handled the concerns by expressing how much he trusted the groups to make excellent decisions, but he also asked the various groups to be sure to send a copy of their minutes to him and the senior lay leadership group.

Paul also found it helpful to spend more time in person with the few people who seemed particularly upset. By being creative, he was able to find ways to accompany them in their daily routine or include them in his visiting in the mission field. Paul discovered that by focusing his energy in handling a complaint with love and understanding rather than dispute and conquest, the level of tension in the congregation and within himself dropped precipitously.

As the fall months progressed, preparation of next year's budget provided an opportunity for Paul to broach the subject of the congregation's mission. First, he privately discussed with a few influential members the concept of having the annual budget reflect the congregation's ministry direction. All agreed that the congregation really did not have a ministry direction other than continuing what had been done the prior year.

With Paul's encouragement and the support of a few key leaders, the senior leadership group decided to ask for help from someone outside the congregation. David provided Paul with a list of the denomination's staff, along with other individuals who help congregations in that way. The leaders decided to follow David's suggestion and looked for consultants who worked with the whole congregation.

The assistance resulted in a mission plan created by the entire congregation. More importantly, because the entire congregation developed the mission plan, it was implemented immediately. Because the entire congregation created the mission plan, the plan did not just sit on a shelf. Instead the action teams identified in the plan had their first meetings during the week following the planning weekend. For both Paul and the congregation, it was an igniting experience.

As the next two years progressed, both Paul and the congregation grew. They grew spiritually and missionally. They came together as a united body of Christ responding to Jesus' invitation to be active in the Great Commission by creating disciples.

> "For God so loved the WORLD,"
> not for God so loved the church.

Paul remembered a key passage from his search to choose between internal and mission focus. John 3:16 provided him with a clear direction. The passage says, "For God so loved the world that he sent His only begotten son."

Paul had made a small sign that helped him maintain focus through the myriad of diversions in the life of a parish pastor. He kept the sign near his office phone and a smaller version in his day planner.

Great Commission is about mission,
    not meetings.
Spiritual development occurs rapidly in
    people who are in mission.
A pastor who is not in mission cannot
    expect members to be in mission.

Paul found a renewed sense of ministry. He was no longer plagued by sleepless nights. Confrontation in the congregation virtually vanished. Everyone did not always agree. However, by maintaining focus on ministry, differences of opinion were channeled into improving ministry ideas rather than tearing people down.

Paul discovered that being a healing leader was more fun and more helpful than being a controlling leader. Paul found his way to peace and mission. The congregation discovered its path to the next level of ministry. Both the pastor and the congregation experienced a new beginning in ministry.

God is good. We are blessed to participate in the Great Commission.

A Prayer by Kennon Callahan
God of mission and of mystery,
God of grace and of galaxies,
    of salvation,
        and solar systems,

God of hope,
    light years, new stars,
God of all that is here
    and all that is beyond,
We are grateful for your compassion
    with us.

The immensity of the universe
    teaches us the immensity
        of your love for us.
Stir our strengths.
    Touch our lives.

The worst of us
    is in the best of us.
The best of us
    is in the worst of us.

Cleanse the worst from within us.
    Forgive our feeble sins.
        Have mercy on our terrible sins.

Help us to live beyond
    our low self-esteem.
Still our compulsiveness
    toward perfectionism.
Release our anger.
    Lift our depression.

Grow forward the best within us.

Grant us wisdom and judgment.
       Give us vision and common sense.
       Let our lives be filled with prayer.

Stir our passion.
       Deepen our compassion.
May your grace be to us a drenching rain
       that gives new life.

May we sense the living,
       moving spirit of your presence
            with us now.

Call us to mission.
       Help us answer your call.

           In Jesus' name.
           Amen

Sources of Assistance

Change from churched to unchurched culture
The Once and Future Church, Loren B. Mead
(ISBN 1-56699-050-5)
In Search of the Unchurched, Alan C. Klaas
(ISBN 1-56699-169-2)

Great Commission-focused ministry
Twelve Keys to an Effective Church, Kennon L. Callahan
(ISBN 0-7879-3871-8)
Purpose Driven Church, Rick Warren (ISBN 0-301-22901-4)
Kicking Habits, Thomas G. Bandy (ISBN 0-687-03189-3)

Conflict in the church
Discovering Your Conflict Management Style, Speed B. Leas
(ISBN 1-56699-184-6)

Missional leadership
Effective Church Leadership, Kennon L. Callahan
(ISBN 0-7879-3865-3)
Overcoming the Dark Side of Leadership, Gary L. McIntosh
and Samuel D. Rima, (ISBN 0-801-09047-4)

Visiting
Visiting in an Age of Mission, Kennon L. Callahan
(ISBN 0-7879-3868-8)

New beginnings at the current or future church
   A New Beginning for Pastors and Congregations, Kennon L.
      Callahan (ISBN 0-7879-4289-8)

Encouragement for ministry wives and women in leadership
   Just Between Us, (a quarterly magazine), Subscription Orders,
      777 S. Barker Road, Brookfield, WI 53045, 800-290-3342

Growing your life forward
   LifeKeys, Jane A.G. Kise, David Stark, and Sandra Krebs Hirsh
      (ISBN 1-55661-871-9)
   Twelve Keys for Living, Kennon L. Callahan
      (ISBN 0-7879-4140-9)

Steps in Transforming from Internal Focused to a Great Commission Focus

Several reviewers of early manuscripts pointed out the difficulty of transforming ministry. Often the forces seeking to retain ministry as if it were still 1950 are very strong and difficult to overcome. A number of ways exist to help congregations and middle-level judicatories accomplish ministry transformation. This appendix provides a summary of the basic concepts and activities. These approaches are effective and can be emulated.

Congregations

Two factors are important in helping a congregation make the transformation. The first factor surfaced in a study that asked sixty-four congregations to describe what in their history caused the transformation to their Great Commission focus. While the specifics were different, most of their stories described a specific, ministry-changing event with two general themes:

1. Virtually the entire congregation was affected, and
2. The event changed the congregation's primary understanding of ministry.

Some of these "Ignitor Events" were positive, like a new pastor, a new facility, or new ministry capability. Others were negative events, such as an indiscretion, the need to relocate, or in one case the sanctuary was hit by lightning and burned to the ground. All these different instances provided a spark that created so powerful a fire for the Great Commission that resistance melted away.

The second factor is that congregations need to experience a sequence of connected understandings. There are six basic concepts that must be grasped before transformation is possible.

These concepts must be internalized **in the order listed**. Well-meaning ministry leaders or consultants attempt to skip important early steps and go directly to implementing changes. This is the main reason so many ministry plans and consultant reports sit on shelves gathering dust.

The steps are:

1. **Accept that we no longer live in a "churched culture."**
    Simply looking around every day would seem to make this an obvious step. Unfortunately, many churched people see their congregation as a refuge from the outside world, or are so involved within their church as a sanctuary that the impact of the world is barely noticed. If people do not overtly accept this first step, they will not understand and will resist anything that follows.

2. **Understand the differences between the "churched culture" and the current "unchurched culture."**
    While most people have a general awareness that times have changed, they need to know the specific differences in order to comprehend the coming steps.

3. **Understand the impact of the changed culture on their local congregation.**
    Amazingly, few congregation members are aware of how much the ministry has deteriorated over the past ten or twenty years. They are generally aware that things are not what they used to be, but they are too busy trying to keep things going to notice what is actually happening. Simply displaying a chart of average weekly worship attendance

over ten or twenty years helps congregations understand that without changing, they will eventually get where they are headed.

4. **Understand that the church must function differently to be effective in the current "unchurched culture."**
This again may seem obvious. It is not. Many people recall with awe the glory days of the churched culture. They use phrases like "we simply need to work harder" or "we just need more commitment." Neither is helpful in the unchurched society.

5. **Accept that the congregation must change.**
The members of the congregation as a whole must come to feel invigorated by the prospect of becoming a Great Commission congregation. This step can only be accomplished by the whole congregation. Trouble always follows when the pastor or a few key leaders attempt to introduce change before the whole congregation has progressed through the first four steps and then together chosen to change its focus.

6. **Decide to become a Great Commission congregation.**
The congregation, as a whole, not acting upon recommendation from some council or committee, creates a missional ministry plan for the coming three to five years. It selects the specific activities to implement and creates action teams to take action.

Congregations can change when they experience an "ignitor event." However, an "ignitor event" only happens with the whole congregation, not a small group or a few key leaders. "Whole congregation" means twenty to forty percent of the average weekly worship attendance—regardless of the congregation's size.

Two types of activity create effective "ignitor events." Congregations that are reasonable healthy and without old issues can usually skip the first activity.

Situation Assessment

The "Situation Assessment" uses individual and group sessions to interview all available leaders and many active members. These interviews reveal true attitudes and feelings about the congregation's ministry. The last day should feature a presentation that is customized to what was heard during the listening sessions. The presentation is to the whole congregation, including all leaders. The presentation:

1. Holds up a mirror of struggling congregations.
2. Holds up a mirror of thriving ministries.
3. Asks the congregation to reflect on which mirror they currently see themselves in and which image makes the best sense for them in the future.

This activity leaves the entire congregation, not just the leaders and the few people who show up for the voters' meeting, in a position to make an informed decision about its future.

The "Situation Assessment" achieves Step 1 through Step 4. It concludes with the congregation making a preliminary decision about Step 5.

Congregation Ignitor Event

When the congregation decides to be a Great Commission congregation, the next step is to create a plan. The entire congregation creates the mission plan. The process takes place in the form of a "Congregation Ignitor Event," held on a Friday evening and Saturday.

During the "Congregation Ignitor Event," the congregation (twenty to forty percent of weekly worship attendance) will:

1. Complete a realistic assessment of the congregation's situation.
2. Create a vision for the future direction of the congregation.
3. Assess the congregation in twelve key areas of ministry.
4. Select specific areas to work on in the coming three to five years, complete with timelines and objectives.
5. Create action teams that implement the plan **starting the following Monday.**

The "Congregation Ignitor Event" quickly reviews Step 1 through Step 4. It concentrates on Steps 5 and 6.

After completing the transformation to a Great Commission congregation, some parishes are able to continue to progress as the Lord leads them. Others secure our assistance in the areas of:

- Creating a new constitution and bylaws (accomplished in one Saturday session with the entire congregation).
- Creating a formal lay mobilization system (a one-day or two-day conference with key leaders).
- Leadership development training for the paid and volunteer leaders (often a weekend retreat).
- "Visiting in an Age of Mission" using Kennon Callahan's wonderful insights for the visitation outreach team (usually an evening event).
- Customized assistance as needed.

Middle-Level Judicatories

Middle-level judicatories are the formal structures that exist between the denomination and local congregations. Some denominations have one while others have two middle-level structures. We primarily work with the group closest to the congregations.

Judicatories have to go through the same six-step process as congregations. Those involved generally are aware of the effect of

Steps 1 through 3 on congregations, but have not made the connection to how the changes affect judicatories. The judicatory leaders need to translate the large amount of information written and widely available about congregational change into implications for judicatory change.

Paid and volunteer judicatory leaders also need help discovering those things they need to do differently. Steps 4 through 6 are new territory for judicatory leaders because very little is written about judicatory transformation. Many judicatories are so steeped in traditional activities they forget the observation that, "Insanity is doing the same thing over and over and expecting a different result."

While some situations and traditions require modifications, the activities needed to accomplish judicatory transformation fall into the same sequence as for congregations.

Great Commission Initiative Event

This weekend event provides an unlimited number of congregations the opportunity to learn about becoming a mission outpost on their local mission field. It results in eighty percent of congregations committing to specific plans of action, with ninety percent actually implementing the plan.

Congregation Ignitor Event Training

This weekend event trains teams of at least four people from an unlimited number of congregations to conduct their own congregation ignitor event described in the "Congregations" section above.

Workshop on Judicatory Change

A retreat-type workshop teaches paid and volunteer leaders the specific ways in which the change to an "unchurched culture" that has so profoundly affected congregations has also impacted judicatories. The workshop describes the changes other judicatories have made and the levels of success they have achieved. It helps those responsible understand why the judicatory struggles and what can be done to achieve Great Commission ministry success.

Congregation Listening Posts

Virtually all judicatories see themselves as servants to the congregations. As such, it is powerful for the member congregations to guide the judicatory transformation process. This has the accompanying advantage of assuring that any needed changes in judicatory structure will be widely supported by the congregations. The rule of thumb is, "When the final vote is taken it will have been a foregone conclusion."

The judicatory conducts a sequence of two listening posts. In the first, members from all congregations in a geographic area gather to describe their ministries and the kind of help they need. The second listening post is a few months later. Congregation members gather to review all the needed ministry assistance, hear a description of the themes that emerged, and react to insights about structure that surfaced.

These insights form the basis for structural changes to the judicatory.

Revised Judicatory Constitution and Bylaws

The final step in helping judicatories is guidance through the writing, approval, and organizational details of changing to a Great Commission structure. The details emerge from the Congregation

Listening Posts and experience with developments pioneered by other judicatories. The process is different for each judicatory.

Those interested in hearing more about these procedures can contact:

www.MissionGrowth.org
or
AlanKlaas@aol.com
or
816-873-3701

Book Order Form
(Photocopy for Future Use)

Sometimes readers desire to refer a book to others. The next page contains an order form and information about how to place an order. Copying the form for use will make the original available for future referrals.

Substantial discounts are available for ordering larger quantities of any combination of the listed books. The details are provided at the ↵ in the middle of the order form.

Book Order Form
(Photocopy for Future Use)

	Price	Quantity	Total per Book
Quiet Conversations	$16 x	_____	= _____
In Search of the Unchurched	$16 x	_____	= _____
Missional Constitution/Bylaws	$16 x	_____	= _____

(Shipped after November 1, 2000)

Total books ordered and amount _____ _____ A

Discount on total books ordered ←——————┐
6 – 19 books, deduct 20%
20 or more books, deduct 40% – $ _____ B

Missouri addresses add 6% of A - B for sales tax + _____ C

Shipping & handling + __$4.50_ D

Express shipping, add $15 + _____ E

TOTAL (combine A, B, C, D, & E) _____

MasterCard or VISA number: _____

Expiration Date: _____

Name on card: _____

Phone: _____ Email:_____

Ship to: _____

_____

FAX order: 816-873-3404
Web site order: www.MissionGrowth.org
Telephone order: 800-260-7966
Mail order (and check): *Mission Growth Publishing*
                    PMB 165
                    13 NW Barry Road
                    Kansas City, MO 64155-2728